Your Career Sucks

But It Doesn't Have To

Daniel Hampton

DANIEL HAMPTON

Copyright © 2018 Daniel Hampton

All rights reserved.

ISBN-13: 978-1-7266-3006-1

YOUR CAREER SUCKS

DANIEL HAMPTON

CONTENTS

	Introduction	6
0.	Be Competent	11
1.	Get Things Done	14
2.	Make Your Manager's Life Easy	23
3.	Communicate	35
4.	Follow Through	46
5.	Take Goals Seriously	52
6.	Leave The Role Better Than You Found It	57
7.	Never Stop Making Yourself More Valuable	62
8.	Share The Success	69
9.	Cultivate Good Relationships And Communication	73
10.	Respect Everyone's Time	79
11.	Know When To Make A Change	84
	Conclusion	91
	Appendix	92

YOUR CAREER SUCKS

Introduction

I don't want to be a CEO. I'm not particularly interested in corporate politics or climbing the ladder or how my salary compares to that of my coworker. The most meaningful parts of my life have always existed independently of my job, and I have consistently found that letting work take over too much makes me unhealthy and unhappy. A fulfilling career is something different for everyone, and it is important to find a balance that works well for you.

My balance leans more heavily toward my life outside of the office. I do, however, feel strongly that if I'm going to do something for nine hours a day, then I'm going to do it well. If your ultimate career goal is to see how far you can move up the corporate structure, then this book isn't for you. If your focus is working hard, getting paid well for it, and maintaining a healthy balance between your personal life and work, then you're in the right place.

Over the last ten years, I have worked in software development for teams and organizations of various sizes on a myriad of different projects. I entered the workforce with a degree in computer science, and while it prepared me well for the technical challenges I would face, I discovered very quickly that there was a whole world of other skills to which I had never been exposed and needed to learn. Expert level technical ability only buys limited career success.

Early in my career, I was often frustrated because it seemed like the people who were really doing the work consistently received less recognition and reward than those who talked a big game but didn't actually do much. It felt like my perception of value and the organization's perception of value were vastly different, and I eventually realized that my observation was absolutely correct. I needed to understand what the company valued if I was going to be successful.

Fortunately, I have been very lucky to work with a number of great mentors (both formal and informal) over the years who have helped me to acquire the skills that I lacked when I graduated from college. I've also learned a lot of things the hard way. Over time, I have established a few repeatable habits that reliably help me work more effectively by doing the stuff I didn't know was important at the start of my career.

As with most things, I think the proof is in the results. So far I have enjoyed exactly the career I wanted. I have consistently received above average performance reviews, good bonuses, and raises. I have been given the opportunity to be more involved in the hiring process and have had the chance to develop new team processes. I have also had the chance to mentor coworkers and have formed amazing long term friendships. Outside of work, I have been able to travel with my wife, play in bands, maintain good relationships with family, start a podcast, and write.

I have seen a lot of good people, though, who are not happy with their career. They are hard workers who contribute significantly to their team, are well regarded by their coworkers, and are consistently passed over for good ratings, raises, promotions, and bonuses. Many times someone in this situation will think that the answer is to work harder and put in more hours. This results in more stress and less time spent doing the things that they enjoy outside of work... but without any improvement. This book is for those people.

If you feel stuck in your career, then you probably are. If you are putting in extra hours but feel like it's not paying off, then it probably isn't. If you feel like you've tried everything you can think of but are still not getting promoted or offered new opportunities, then you've come to the right place. Take heart. Your career sucks, but you can fix it!

Key Concepts:

There are two key concepts that will come up over and over again in this book: perception and reputation. Before we get started, I would like to provide some more detail about what those terms mean (at least to me).

Perception
A lot of what I talk about in this book is aimed at helping you shape the way

that others in your organization see you and your work. A lot of times an employee who works hard does not see a proportional amount of recognition and advancement simply because the people who make decisions about those sorts of things have no visibility into that employee's contributions. For long term career success, working hard is essential. It is, however, equally important that others are aware of your hard work and how it adds value. It takes deliberate effort to make this happen. That is what I mean when I talk about shaping perception.

Visibility is one important piece of success, but the other piece is making sure that what you do adds value in a way that is perceived as contributing to the larger goals of the company. I have encountered several people in my career who are always busy but never on the things that most benefited the organization's success. A lot of this book will be focused on making sure you are correctly aligned on how to prioritize your efforts. When your work is the right work and the decision makers at your company are aware of it, then you are setting yourself up for long term career success.

As a quick aside, while there is no dedicated chapter on this, please be very wary of actions or habits that create a negative perception. Try to evaluate your day to day activities through the lens of a manager from another department. Are you doing anything that would create a negative impression on someone from another team walking by your work area? Are you on your phone during meetings? Are you browsing Reddit or Facebook regularly at work? Do you routinely show up late to meetings? While all of these actions may be completely normal and acceptable in your group, keep in mind that your perception is something that extends beyond your own team.

Reputation

Another key to long term career success is your reputation. Over time, you will become known for certain traits and attributes. You can probably think of a past (or present) coworker who was known for being stubborn or resistant to change. You can probably also think of a past coworker who everyone knows as the type of person who just gets things done. Your reputation is usually known by more people than interact with you directly. It can take on a life of its own over time, and people who make decisions about raises, bonuses, and advancement are not unaware of it. Therefore, reputation is something you need to be deliberate about.

Reputation is not something to lose sleep over. Coming in and working hard every day is a great place to start. Getting the job done and working well with others tends to shape your reputation in a good way, and if you are reading this book, then you are probably already doing that. Sometimes, though, if you do not pay attention, your reputation can grow in ways you did not intend. For example, if over the course of five years you turn down three potential role changes (for three perfectly valid reasons), then you may start to develop the reputation of someone who does not embrace change or is not looking for new opportunities. To offset this, you can make sure to volunteer for new projects, additional responsibilities in your current role, etc. Nothing difficult - just something of which you should be mindful. A lot of the following chapters will give more specific ways to help build your reputation in the way you want.

General Notes:

Target audience
The target audience for this book is individual contributors or team leads working white collar jobs. This has been my world for the last ten years. I worked in restaurants and mowed lawns during high school and college, but I didn't spend enough time in those vocations to really figure out any keys to success beyond showing up on time and working hard. I'm sure some of the principles can be applied to other environments, but I'll be sticking to what I know as far as examples.

This book is also targeted toward hard workers. This is not advice for how to cheat the system or to get away with something. The point of the following chapters is to help you understand how your employer sees you, figure out what your organization values, and communicate effectively what you are contributing. If you are looking for shortcuts, then this is not the book for you. If you are looking for advice on how to get credit for what you are already doing, then you are in the right place.

Examples
Since my whole career has been spent in software development, that is the context in which all my experience takes place. None of the principles I have documented in this book are at all specific to technology or software development, but many of the examples I use will take place in that context. I'll do my best to generalize them, but please keep in mind that the point of each example is the general concept that it demonstrates, not the technical minutiae.

Order
Aside from "Chapter 0", the order of the chapters does not matter. They are each meant to be self-contained pieces of advice that can completely stand alone. Each chapter is also formatted in such a way that you can read it and

immediately take action based on the information. If you want to pick a chapter that addresses a current struggle, work on getting that under control, and then come back to the rest of the book later, that's totally fine. All of the chapters are meant to flow together and complement each other, but the book does not need to be read in its entirety for you can start taking advantage of the ideas presented.

The appendix
An appendix is included at the end of the book with practical examples of applying each chapter's principles to common workplace scenarios. If you would like to read some of these first to get an idea of what this book is about, then feel free! Keep in mind that these examples are focused very much on the "what" and not the "why", though.

0. Be Competent

I labeled this as Chapter 0 because it is the most important. It is so important, in fact, that its absence would make all other chapters of this book irrelevant. This will also be the harshest chapter because everything in the rest of the book presumes the following three sentences:

You cannot be successful without being competent. There is no magic shortcut. If you are not qualified to do your job (or are at least making a momentous effort to get there), then no amount of coaching or advice will overcome that.

For the sake of this discussion, competency means possessing the basic skills needed to perform the tasks required for your job. If you are a software developer, you better know how to write code. If you are in Human Resources, then you better know your company's vacation policy inside and out. If you are an accountant, then you should certainly know your way around debits and credits. If you do not have the basic skills required to do your job, then you will not build a successful career, and none of the advice in this book will help you in the long run.

Not everyone in the world is a technical genius. Not everyone has the time (or passion) required to perfect the craft they do as a day job. Everyone can, however, make the time to be competent. If you are not interested enough in your field to put in the effort to be proficient at it, then you need to change jobs. Now. You are not positioning yourself for long term success, and you need to find a profession where you can. Your job should at least be interesting enough that you enjoy learning the skills that are required for it, and you should feel a sense of accomplishment as you learn them.

You are rarely expected to know everything on day one, but you should at least come in to a new role with some baseline knowledge and start working toward excellence immediately. Sometimes this requires work on your part outside of the office. This is okay once in a while, but do not let it become an expectation. Time management is one of the most important skills you will ever develop. If you do not know where to start with getting up to speed on something, then ask someone with more experience. When others see that you are applying yourself, they are almost always willing to help.

Since graduating college, I have changed jobs several times. Every time has been equal parts terrifying, exciting, and humbling. Transitioning from being someone who primarily answers questions for others to being someone who primarily asks questions of others is a bit of an ego hit. Keeping a good attitude, taking good notes, and learning quickly are fast ways to help form good relationships with others on your team. These relationships then become a great asset for learning how to best direct your efforts. It should not take long for you to get to the point where you can start contributing.

Changing jobs is not the only time this matters, though. The title of this chapter is "Be Competent" rather than "Become Competent", because it is not a one-time event. After you become competent, you need to actively stay that way. Every industry goes through changes, but so do the needs of your team and larger organization. Make sure that you keep an eye out for what changes are on the horizon and be proactive about getting ahead of the curve. Again, this may take some investment outside of your normal working hours, but be smart about it and invest when you need to. Never stop learning, but be efficient as you do it. Again, people who are more experienced in your field are great resources for getting direction on what you should be learning.

To do your job and have long term success, you must at least be competent. You do not, however, need to be a technical rock star with ten years of experience in your field to succeed or perform at a high level. As long as you are competent and are always working at getting better, then no one can complain about your level of skill. Competency is the bare minimum for success. There are, however, a lot of things beyond it that can make you stand out and be considered for advancement and additional opportunities. The rest of this book will focus on those things.

YOUR CAREER SUCKS

1. Get Things Done

Based on my experience, people are generally pretty good at working on a project or task. What they are not good at is starting or ending a project or task. I could speculate about reasons for this (I think there are psychological reasons and also process reasons…), but what it really comes down to is that for whatever reason, most people seem to make way more progress in the middle of a project than they do at the beginning or the end. That said, beginnings and endings of projects/tasks/assignments/whatever are situations with great visibility and potential for impact.

You probably have coworkers who always seem to be working but never seem to deliver anything. Or maybe you find yourself falling into that category. I think that one disconnect comes in how workers view work vs how managers view work. For example, if I make significant progress on four different tasks today but fail to complete something that my manager sees as a high priority, I am likely to see my day as productive… but my manager probably will not.

It is easy to work on something when you have all the information you need to be able to make progress. What is difficult is actively gathering the information you need to move things forward. It is also difficult to push something through processes that you do not have complete control over. It is tempting to walk away from a task when you have solved the problem, but the important thing to remember is that no one else sees the task as done at that point. To the outside observer, you get way more credit for completing a task than you do for moving it along significantly.

The beginning of a project sets the tone for everything to come. It is a time when expectations are set for the timeline, roles, deliverables, frequency of meetings, etc. Being involved and taking on a leadership role at the beginning of a project gives you the opportunity to set yourself and your team up for success. If you do not provide the roadmap, then someone else will, and that someone else often doesn't know what's reasonable to expect. If you do not define processes and what "done" means, then you're likely to find yourself operating on someone else's schedule and being measured against whatever their idea of success is at any given moment for any given task.

Once a project has been defined, it can often be intimidating to know where to start. This is especially difficult if you do not already know how to do all the things you will need to do to complete it. A lot of people will spin their wheels working on less critical tasks that they already know how to do, rather than getting themselves up to speed on what they need to know for the higher priority items. Do not make this mistake. The best way to learn is by doing, so trust yourself and your ability to learn and jump in head first.

Tracking progress during a project can also be difficult. Many people like to spend as little time as possible on this and get annoyed when they are asked how something is going. I prefer to set incremental milestones purely in terms of demonstrable deliverables and then give approximate dates for when they could reasonably be done. If one of the deliverables is creeping past that point, then it is a good time for everyone to reevaluate and potentially take action to unblock whatever is holding things up. This provides more visibility into what is really going on and helps the team work together more effectively. Investing a small amount of time early on to get everyone aligned on a plan of attack pays off for the whole duration of the project and leaves fewer loose ends to try and tie up at the end.

Here are some concrete things you can do with the next task or project you receive so that you can start making progress quickly, measure that progress, and then move it to completion and off your plate:

Figure out a definition of "done".
One of the most important things you can do when starting any task or project is figure out a definition of "done". Clearly writing down what a finished product looks like is a great way to keep yourself on target, and it also helps others know what to expect from you when you say that something has been completed. It amazes me how in a meeting, everyone in the room can perceive the word "done" to mean something different. This leads to all kinds of issues that can be easily avoided with a little work ahead of time.

A good definition of done helps you stay focused on the task at hand. Like the picture on the cover of a puzzle box, it constantly reminds you what you are working toward, and should bring focus and help eliminate distractions.

Most responsible professionals also take some amount of pride in their work. This is great, but it can lead to a strong tendency toward scope creep. It's easy to talk yourself into one more feature, one more refactor, one more admin tool, etc. Make sure to specify what is NOT included in your definition of done so that you cannot talk yourself into delaying delivery.

Documenting your own definition of done is also a good communication tool. Make it available on a wiki or other collaboration site. Your project manager, team members, manager, and customers will all know exactly what you mean when you say that a task is complete, and this is amazingly helpful. If nothing else, it will give everyone else a chance to clarify requirements and expectations from the outset as opposed to on the day of the deadline when you think that you've done everything you were supposed to do.

A next level step is to define a common definition of done for your whole team. If you're on a team of developers or a mixed-specialty project team, then it is valuable to have a common definition of done for customers, project managers, or supervisors. The effects of doing this as an individual are magnified when an entire team can adopt it. It helps you and your coworkers keep each other accountable and removes the need for wasted time on internal discussions about the state of any particular task. Being the one to introduce this concept and get buy in from your team is the type of thing that your manager and coworkers will notice and appreciate.

A good definition of done will have the following characteristics:

- Establishes scope (refers to a requirements document or contract or spells it out)
- Includes enough information for someone else to know what needs to be done next without asking you
- Makes it clear what will NOT be done (Ex. "I will be ready to present my findings when asked" means that you do not plan to schedule a meeting to discuss your findings.)

Here are two examples of a definition of done for a team:

Technical: When we say that a task is done, we mean that the coding has been completed in a way that meets all of the requirements to the best of our understanding. The new code has 80+% unit test coverage and enough documentation in the readme file for a new developer to get things up and running on their machine in a timely manner. The changes have been merged into a release branch. The code in that branch has been tested on our pre-dev environment without issue and is ready for the QA team to deploy into the staging environment and perform regression testing. We will not have assigned a version number or integrated any bug fixes that may be pending for the version of code that is currently in production.

Non-Technical: When we say that a lawn is done, we mean that both the front and back have been mowed and edged. Any additional landscaping work (agreed upon at least 24 hours in advance and documented in the work order) has been completed, and all visible grass clippings and spilled mulch have been removed from the yard. The work order has been filled out with our start and finish time and placed in the envelope that gets returned to the main office each night. A receipt was placed on the front porch of the home before we left. Any damaged equipment was reported via email to John on the same day as the job on which it was damaged.

Here are two examples of a definition of done for an individual:

Technical: When I say that my task to write a new timesheet application is done, I will mean that all of the coding is complete and deployed into the development environment. I will have 80+% unit test coverage, and will have performed a basic level of integration testing. Any merge conflicts will have been resolved. The Testing team will have been notified that the new app is ready for testing. If I encountered any bugs in the existing code base while working on this new feature, they will have been documented on the team's bugs list with enough information to recreate. Any ideas for future enhancements to the new timesheet application will be documented and added to our product backlog.

Non-Technical: When I say that my task to gather information about the best way to provide coffee for the office is complete, I will mean that I have explored various sources (both in print and in person) and selected three options that would seem most practical for our situation. I will have completed a proof of concept for each and will be able to provide samples for a taste test (with 24 hours notice). I will also have completed a yearly cost estimate for each and documented it in our office wiki page. When the wiki page is complete, I will notify my supervisor and then be available for follow up meetings or taste tests as needed.

Find something you can start doing today.
Starting a task is hard and intimidating. In software development, it is often impractical to wait until someone has given you all the requirements you will need before you start working. There are also many scenarios where a project will rely on you learning to do something you do not know how to do yet. That's okay. The important thing is to start doing something that gets you

closer to being done.

It is not uncommon for people who are not in your discipline to request something from you without giving you all the information you need to do it. This makes sense. If you do not write software all day, then you probably do not have a very good understanding of what sorts of information you need in order to be able to write software. Sitting around and waiting for someone else to magically learn to gather the type of information you need is not a good way to get things done. You will accomplish much more (and have better working relationships) if you are proactive about your needs.

If you have incomplete requirements, try scheduling a meeting about one specific aspect of the project that seems to be self-contained or close to definite. Go through the exercise of getting the type of specific requirements you need from your customer or business analyst or stakeholder. Narrowing the scope and talking through one specific piece of the project helps provide focus and also helps them understand what level of detail you'll need for the rest of the requirements. It will also allow you to walk out of the meeting with all the information you need to get started on that particular part of the project.

If your career is anything like mine has been, then you will routinely be asked to do something that you do not know how to do or assigned a task that requires a skill set that you do not have. I have noticed that a lot of people react to this by stalling or trying to pass the responsibility to someone else. This is a direct contradiction to the "Get Things Done" mindset. It also sets you up to be in a position where you will have to learn something in an unreasonable amount of time later on to try and hit a deadline, and the quality of your work will suffer.

If you want to perform at a high level throughout your career, you will constantly need to learn new skills. On a large project, one of the biggest challenges is deciding where to focus. One tactic that I have found to be particularly effective is to break any problem or task down into sub-problems and then to attack them one at a time. Typically when venturing into the unknown, I try to identify the smallest self-contained task and then attack it first. It feels good to start making progress, you end up with a deliverable very quickly, and you learn a lot along the way.

For example, I am not a particularly handy person. If I were asked to assemble a set of bedroom furniture, I would begin with the simplest piece (maybe a nightstand) first and completely finish it before starting something else. I would probably watch a couple of YouTube videos and buy or borrow any tools I anticipated needing and then get started. In assembling the nightstand, I would learn a lot about how to read the instructions from the company who produced the furniture, I would know what tools I needed, and I would be dealing with the fewest pieces possible (in case I needed to take it apart and start over at some point). The same principles can be applied to painting a house, building a software application, or repairing a car.

No matter what your task is, look for an attainable subtask, do what you need to do to be able to get started, and then do it. If you wait to have everything you could ever anticipate needing before you start a task, then your work will pile up, and you will learn very little. Narrow the scope, learn what you need to learn, and then deliver something. If it is not perfect on the first try, that's totally okay. It is much better to have a small piece of work that needs to be revisited later than to deliver an entire application in "first draft" quality.

Set milestones.
I mentioned in the previous section that my typical approach to solving a large or complex problem is to break it down into smaller problems, pick the simplest or closest to "ready to work on" one, and then get started. While it is important to get started sooner rather than later, it's also important to plan for the future. One of the most beneficial exercises you can engage in when starting a large task or project is to create a list of milestones and share it with your stakeholders. A list of milestones is beneficial, because it facilitates a conversation about priorities and dependencies.

If you're working by yourself, then creating a list of milestones helps you think through the big picture of what you're trying to accomplish and where the trouble spots might be. For example, if I know that I'm going to need a new web server before the end of the project and that at my company it usually takes at least two weeks to get a web server, then it is probably important to request that server more than two weeks before I need it. This is also a good way of helping pace yourself and know that you are on track for meeting your deadlines.

If you are working with a team, then it helps each person think about the big picture and not just their individual part. For example, if I know that one of my tasks needs to be completed before several of my teammates can complete tasks that they have, then I know to prioritize that task above the others. Talking through all of the dependencies ahead of time can help everyone understand how their actions impact others and lead to a healthier team environment.

Aside from making you look more proactive and organized, a list of milestones is also a very useful communication tool between you and your stakeholders. No one enjoys constant pulse meetings or being pestered for status updates while they try to work. These things are annoying and are really only necessary when people do not understand what needs to be done, where you are in the process, or when they can expect to see results. A list of milestones (with rough delivery dates) provides all of these things.

Many times stakeholders in a project do not even know the right questions to ask to truly determine if things are moving along at a healthy rate. By providing a list of milestones, you are giving them a road map for the project. This gives you a common set of landmarks to use in your discussions and also helps them understand the importance of tasks that are more abstract. For example, if I tell a business analyst that I completed the Dockerfile for a container that will host the API I'm writing, that will probably not get them excited or make them feel like progress is being made. If, however, they can see on the list of milestones that the Dockerfile was needed before being able to see live data in the front end of the app, then they are more likely to be excited by the accomplishment.

Milestones give your stakeholders a way to communicate more effectively with you as well. A project owner probably is not going to give you a lot of helpful feedback on code architecture or the nuances of your trade. What they can do, though, is talk to you about what milestones are important to them and why. If the landing page of a new website is the most important thing for them because they know they will have to get approval from multiple levels of management before it can go live, then that may move getting a mockup of that page to them higher on the priority list than it might otherwise be. This sets you up for success because it gives you common terminology with your customers and can spark discussions that lead to mutually beneficial outcomes.

A list of milestones can also help you coordinate efforts. Do not be afraid to include tasks that are beyond your control on the list. Project managers are great at checking on the status of things, so if you have requested something from another team or another company that is necessary for your project, then make sure that the dependency is listed in your deliverables. If anyone is dissatisfied with how things are progressing, and they can see that an external dependency is the real roadblock, then they can take on the role of trying to expedite the request while you continue to work on the tasks that are fully in your control.

Once all of the interested parties have and understand your milestones list, the next step is to send out regular status updates that reference it. A map can only be so effective without a "You Are Here" sticker. If your stakeholders regularly receive updates in terms that they understand, then they never have to worry about how things are progressing. It is a very good career move to be known as someone who provides relevant information without having to be asked.

Even though it will take some time and thought, creating a list of high level milestones is a valuable way to start a project. By sharing this list with your team, your leadership, and your customers, you set the tone for communication, collaboration, and the work to come. Whether the list is for you or your whole team, being the one who takes on the primary responsibility of creating it is the type of proactive organizational activity that your manager and even people outside your team will notice. This is the sort of thing that plays well in bonus or promotion discussions.

A good list of milestones should have the following:

- Clear identification of tasks that must be done to enable other tasks
- Clear identification of tasks that can be worked on concurrently
- An owner identified for each milestone (this can be a person or team)
- General enough milestones that all stakeholders can understand them
- Specific enough milestones that they can be delivered regularly (I would recommend no more than a week or two to complete each)
- Enough documentation that everyone is clear about what is included (perhaps even a link to your definition of done)

Putting it all together.
Everything discussed in this section is pretty specific to my own experiences and will necessarily look different depending on the details of your particular job. Hopefully you should be able to take these concepts and apply them in your day to day. Figure out what works best for your situation, and do not be afraid to change things up if anything does not work the way you expect it to on the first try.

The big takeaway here is that people tend to be better at middles than they are at beginnings and endings. For yourself, a good way to manage this is to limit scope, prioritize, and then dig in on the most important thing. Taking time to think through dependencies, agreeing on a path forward, and measuring progress will often spark larger discussions with your manager or team and give you an opportunity to positively impact them as well.

DANIEL HAMPTON

2. Make Your Manager's Life Easy

It is important to understand from the outset that your manager is the conduit between you and the people who make decisions that affect you. Whether it be financial, policy related, regarding strategic direction, or otherwise, many of the decisions that will affect you will not be made with you in the room. To that end, it is very much to your benefit to be on good terms with your manager.

Another important point is that your manager's priorities and your own priorities are probably quite different. You answer to different people. Your bonuses are tied to different types of things. Your day to day is very dissimilar. Other people have very different expectations for you than they do for your manager. One key difference in the nature of the work is that your responsibilities probably tend to be focused on the completion of individual tasks or projects. Your manager's responsibilities encompass less tangible things like coaching individuals, managing a budget, keeping the team functioning in a healthy and efficient manner, and representing the team to other groups and various levels of management.

Combining these two ideas means figuring out what your boss's priorities are and then setting him or her up to succeed. There is a lot more to being a good employee than performing your primary job task at a high level. Being a good employee also means being easy to manage. What this looks like will change based on your boss's priorities and the nature of your work, but there are always some relatively easy steps that you can take to move yourself in the right direction.

Another important thing to keep in mind is that your manager is, in fact, human. This means that he or she is not perfect and has certain habits and preferences that may or may not naturally align with the responsibilities of the job. Not all managers are extroverts. Not all managers have a degree in psychology. Not all managers are even very socially graceful. Rather than focusing on a manager's shortcomings in these areas, an exemplary employee will use their emotional intelligence to take an accurate assessment of their manager and then meet them halfway whenever possible.

Generally, when your manager's life is easy, your life is also easy. When a supervisor sees that you don't need to be babysat, then typically they will not feel the need to babysit you. When you are proactively providing a manager with the information they need to succeed, then they will not feel the need to nag you for status reports. When you consistently provide accurate and timely information, your boss will gain trust for your opinions. Also, we all make mistakes. When you do, your manager is significantly more likely to cut you some slack or give you the benefit of the doubt when you have been an ideal employee in the past.

Here are some specific things you can do to develop a good relationship with your manager:

Don't show up on lists.
Managers hate it when their bosses ask them why something hasn't been done. My first job was for a very large corporation. Someone high up the chain of command believed that it was important for everyone in the company to change their password every 90 days, so every quarter a report would be generated that listed everyone who had not changed their password. I remember my supervisor sending emails every quarter to the team saying that if you were on the list then you needed to change your password. He would mention it in meetings. He would go to individual desks to remind people.

It seemed quite strange to me that something that was so simple for any one employee to do was costing our manager hours of his life every three months. Every minute that my boss spent walking desk to desk or typing up emails to encourage people to be compliant was one minute that he was not spending on spearheading initiatives with other teams, dealing with overly aggressive project managers, or (more importantly) working on the paperwork for my next raise. I resolved at the time that I never wanted to show up on the expired passwords list, and I never did after that. I also decided that I never wanted to show up on any type of non-compliance list. Ever.

You may disagree with corporate policies or due dates. You may not like the performance rating system or the account ownership review rules or the records management initiatives that take place every year or quarter. What you need to understand, though, is that all of these things take you relatively little effort and a lot of other people in your company will blow them off. Every time someone blows it off, it creates bad visibility and wasted time for your manager, and it is an absolute fact that your manager knows it. Do not be part of the problem. Every manager I have every worked for has commented positively on the fact that I do not show up on lists.

Communicate efficiently.
No one likes status reports. Your manager does not like asking for them any more than you like writing them. The problem, though, is that they are a necessary evil. In my experience, they are typically a solution to a larger problem with communication. They do, however, server a purpose and also provide a chance for you to present your work in a way that benefits you.

Your boss does not want you to write status reports simply for extra reading material. The whole concept of a status report (daily/weekly/whatever) is to enforce communication between you and your boss. The fact that this is necessary amongst a group of working adults is kind of sad, but it also presents a great opportunity for you to do more than the bare minimum and make your boss's life significantly easier.

If you are not currently required to write status reports, then one way to keep from having to do them is to proactively provide information when it is needed. Be attuned to your manager's priorities and make sure that they are receiving the information they need in a timely manner. You do not want to communicate so much that it gets tuned out, but you want the information to always be there ahead of when it is needed.

Good communication with your boss has the following traits:

- **Organization:** Group your updates by project or initiative. That way when your manager is asked about the status of that project or initiative, they can quickly find all of the relevant information.
- **Context:** Provide enough context that anyone can know what you're talking about. If your manager forwards your update to a project stakeholder, there should be enough information that they can understand exactly what was done.
- **Value:** Explain why what you did is beneficial. If there's no value, do not report it. Most of the people who read your status updates are interested in the why of your work, not the how.

Do not write status updates like this:

Updated db servers. Set up new testing environment. Created new test accounts. Changed password on functional account.

Do write status updates like this:

Compliance/Support
- *Updated the SQL database servers in our extranet environment with Windows patches to help with performance and to maintain security.*
- *Changed password on the functional account that our team uses for production access to stay in compliance with the security team's password policy.*

Mobile Site Project
- *Set up new test server to be used by the development team to host their new mobile site and gave them access to deploy. Site is only accessible internally and to members of security group xxxxx.*
- *Created several new test accounts for the project team to use for testing various user experiences on the new mobile site.*

One more general note on this point: Make sure that you use your manager's preferred communication style whenever possible. This helps your information be delivered in a way that fits their process and is thus more likely to be absorbed. If your boss religiously checks and responds to email, then that is probably a good way to communicate. If, however, your boss has an inbox with thousands of unopened items and runs meetings off of a team wiki page, then make sure your updates are on the wiki page. Some managers that I have worked with prefer to have frequent one on one meetings and then take their own notes on their laptops. In that situation, I still wrote my status updates in a text file and took them to those meetings to reference. Moral of the story: Be aware of your boss's preferred method of communication and keep them updated in a way that is effective.

Understand your manager's priorities.
An important part of being easy to manage is understanding your manager's priorities. It is very easy to get caught up in the day to day of your job and to focus entirely on what you are expected to do. It is also very easy to feel like you have a good sense of what really needs to be done to keep things running. People who work hard are, in my experience, very susceptible to this. They spend all day heads down in their area of responsibility and develop a deep understanding of what they do. They see the connections and dependencies between tasks and end up with a strong gut feeling for how risky a project is, how disruptive proposed changes will be, and when it is worth spending extra time to research something before implementing it.

This level of expertise and intuition is a great asset for a team, and it is a level you want to reach in your own career. A potential pitfall, though, is that employees in this mindset can very easily lose sight of what is important to their managers. Time and time again I have seen some of the most experienced and technically gifted members of a team also be the most difficult to manage simply because they see their work in a totally different way than their boss does. Managers are held responsible for completely different types of things than individual contributors, and understanding what drives your supervisor is absolutely essential to performing in a way that will be successful in your organization.

Your boss typically has access to more information than you do and much more insight into higher level organizational goals and initiatives. A manager's job is to set priority for work and make sure things get done on time. You may deem something as more important than what your manager has set as the highest priority. This can be frustrating, especially when you have more information about what it takes to actually accomplish the work than they do. However, there are a number of things you can do to help your manager get their job done while you also complete your tasks efficiently.

1. **Inform:** Your manager's job is to decide what needs to get done. You may not have the ability to make those decisions, but you can at least make sure your manager is informed when they are evaluating priorities. I have thus far never been hired (or seen anyone else be hired) to tell a manager "no". I had a project manager who used to say "With enough time and money, anything is possible", and I feel like this is a great mindset to have. As an individual contributor, your role is to give your manager an accurate idea of how much time and money will be required to accomplish any particular initiative. If they understand early what all is involved, then it helps set expectations appropriately and allows them to better balance availability across the team.
2. **Update:** Keep your manager up to date on what is going on with a project. If something unforeseen comes up, then communicate early and often. Project stakeholders and people outside the organization will often ask your supervisor for updates. The higher the visibility of the project or task, the more likely it is that more people will be asking your manager about it. Make sure that they have up to date information about the status of the project in terms of the final deliverable. They do not care about the minutiae of the task execution. They do care about seeing progress toward the end goal and any roadblocks that are currently delaying it.

3. **Check In:** Touch base with your supervisor at least once a week about work currently in progress and what comes next. Ask them what their priorities are, and do not hesitate to change course when necessary. Most people want to finish what they have started. It is natural to crave that feeling of closure on a task or project. One characteristic of a good employee, though, is that they always seem to be working on the right thing. Your manager is the best source of information on what the right thing is.

Be easy to coach.
When your manager is willing to invest time in you, then make it easy for them. Think about things from their perspective and make the most of any interactions you have. Even if the information is not being relayed in a way that you would prefer, take what you can from it, and use it to improve your performance. Just because a manager does not communicate in the way that you would prefer does not mean that he or she does not have valuable information to pass along. Managers have a very different perspective on your performance than you do, and being able to understand that perspective and take action based on it is a key to career success.

Here are some general tips for getting the most out of interactions with your manager:

- **Be approachable.** You have probably worked with people who are gruff and uninviting. You have probably put off talking to them about things because you know it will not be a pleasant experience. There are a million reasons why a person might develop this demeanor and reputation. This undoubtedly hurts their relationships with coworkers, but it can also get in the way of their career. If a manager dreads talking to someone, then they are likely going to receive less frequent coaching and mentoring. Do not give your manager an excuse to not approach you when needed. NOTE: I realize this advice is somewhat vague. Every personality type is different, and "unapproachable" can mean a lot of different things. Just keep "approachability" in mind as you read the rest of the points in this list, and think about how it can all work together in your own situation to help facilitate open communication between you and your manager.
- **Be receptive.** Coaching can be difficult to accept, and many people (managers included) can give it in a way that comes across as accusatory rather than constructive. It is a natural response to try to justify your own actions or to get defensive when someone points out your faults. I would strongly encourage you to let your default mode

be "information gathering" when your manager approaches you with a coaching tip. Do your best to clear your mind, eliminate distractions, and fully process what they are saying. I always take a notebook when I meet with a manager, even if it is just for a quick, unscheduled discussion. If I focus on writing down what they are saying, then it helps me capture the information without bias. I can also easily summarize my notes back to them at the end of the discussion to make sure we are on the same page. Your manager may not be a talented coach or mentor. They do, however, provide a different point of view on your performance that is valuable for your career development. The more you can look past the delivery method and focus on the information, the better off you are. If you feel your boss has perceived something inaccurately, then let them fully explain their perspective before trying to correct it. There may still be valuable information to glean from the points they make.

- **Take action.** The best way that you can encourage your manager to keep giving you useful feedback is to take action on it. Make note of specific things your manager asks you to do or change. Be deliberate about implementing that feedback, and then check in with your manager in a couple of weeks or at your next coaching session to review your progress. When a manager gives coaching advice but doesn't see it implemented, then it is very easy for him or her to see coaching as a waste of time and lose motivation to provide it in the future. Even if you find that your manager's coaching is regarding something that you are already doing, then use the feedback as an outline to frame your next discussion. If the issue is that your boss does not see something that you are already doing, then start documenting specific example of it and then share those in your next meeting. You can also use those examples in your yearly performance results.

When something bad happens, provide an overview and a plan of action.

This section has some overlap with the previous one, but there is one scenario that comes up often enough that I feel like it warrants special attention. When something bad happens, it adds stress to the situation. The more levels of management that are involved, the worse that can be. Stress has a way of cascading down the org chart. When something goes wrong, a lot of people want to either pretend that it did not happen or blame someone or something else for it. Neither of these options help the situation. You can choose to be much more proactive in how you handle the situation and also equip your manager to handle any flack that may come from it.

Your boss should not find out from someone else that something went wrong in an area for which you are responsible. As tempting as it may be to keep something hidden, if there is any chance that anyone may have been impacted by whatever happened, then you need to make sure you are the one bringing it up. Managers hate being asked about something they do not know about - especially if it is something negative. Things will go much more positively for you if you help your manager be prepared for questions. When the first notification that a supervisor receives about an incident comes in the form of an inquiry from one of their superiors and they are unprepared to answer, it does not go well for anyone.

In addition to communicating frequently, good employees are very deliberate about the information they share. In times of stress, managers want something they can report to their managers - not a million details. Blaming someone else or going deeply into the technical details of the incident do not equip your supervisor to answer the types of questions they will receive. What I have found to be most effective is to provide a short, high level overview that anyone in the company should be able to read and understand as well as a plan of action for how to address the situation. It also works well to timebox your next communication with a statement like "The issue is currently being worked, and I will provide a status update in 45 minutes if we have not fixed it by then".

Once an issue is resolved, I will typically send a follow up email with a thorough description of the issue, a list of steps taken to resolve it, and an analysis of the root cause. I will also propose a course of action to either mitigate or prevent the issue from happening again in the future. This may be something as simple as "This issue will continue until we finish upgrading all of our servers. The steps to resolve it have been documented in the team wiki, and I sent the link to the help desk along with some instructions on how to diagnose it". Your proposal could also be much more complex: "In order to prevent this in the future, we are going to implement an additional step in our deployment process where both the business owner and technical resource have to approve the deployment ahead of time so that both sides will have the ability to veto the timing if needed. Additionally, we will be generating a set of integration tests for this application so that in future we can find an issue like this before our customers do." Even if your proposal is not accepted, it shows that you are thinking ahead and learning from the situations rather than making excuses or pretending it is not important.

Consider the following scenarios:

Scenario 1:

Late in the evening, you get a notification that the company's website is down. You immediately open your laptop and start investigating. Your supervisor gets a call from his or her manager and is asked why the company's website is down. This is the first that your supervisor has heard about this, and he or she has to exit the conversation without adding any new information. Then you get a call from your supervisor while you are frantically trying to fix the issue, and you have to stop and explain why they were not notified of the issue. Then your supervisor gets called again and asked for a status update. Then you get another call. And so on.

Scenario 2:
Late in the evening, you get a notification that the company's site is down. You immediately text your supervisor saying that the site is down and that you are investigating and will provide a status update in 30 min. You have time to diagnose the issue and figure out what it will take to fix it. Then you call your supervisor and explain what is going on, what it will take to fix it, and roughly how long it will take to put the fix in place. After the issue is resolved, you call your boss to report that the issue has been resolved and that you will be sending a follow up email with additional detail. Then you send a detailed analysis of what happened along with a proposal for how to address the situation going forward.

Scenario 1 is chaotic and stressful, and everyone walks away feeling like everyone else involved was annoying and/or incompetent. Your supervisor looks unprepared and reactive. You are not working effectively because you are being interrupted, and management gets more and more nervous the longer the site is down. Everyone involved feels like they are not getting information unless they pester someone else for it, and no one knows if they can trust the stability of the site moving forward.

Scenario 2 is what exemplary employees do. The communication is proactive, and everyone has their expectations set from the beginning. At any point, if your supervisor gets a call, they are prepared to answer in an intelligent way. They do not have to interrupt you to get that information, and you can get uninterrupted time to troubleshoot. Organized communication is a good way to deflate high stress situations, and it makes you and your supervisor both look competent and responsible. That is a great perception for people outside your organization to have.

Propose solutions.
An important part of your manager's job is fixing problems. The first step in your manager being able to fix a problem is knowing about it. Being a Yes Man (or Yes Woman) does not help you or your manager. No one likes to deliver bad news, but problems can't be solved when they remain unknown. When there are real issues, showing up and telling your manager that everything is fine wastes your time and theirs.

Most people are good at identifying problems. Some people are so good at it that they are able to complain about literally anything. There is a big difference between simply identifying a problem and actually helping to fix it. Make sure that you develop the reputation of being a problem solver and not of being a complainer. I have made it a personal goal for many years not to complain about something to my manager without also proposing at least a couple of solutions to the problem. Sometimes one of my solutions will be implemented and sometimes not. The important thing, though, is that I am coming to the table asking for helping working through something as opposed to just being negative.

Here are some tips for talking to your manager about problems or issues.

- **Focus on processes, not people.** A lot of the issues you experience in the workplace are going to be due to a coworker, but it is not useful to make personal attacks. Managers are not babysitters, and they should not need to waste time on minor personality quirks and conflicts. Where a manager should get involved, though, is when there is something keeping the team from working as effectively as it could. Focus on team-wide process and impact rather than on individual actions. For example, "Karen shows up late to our morning status meeting every day, and it's annoying to rehash everything to get her up to speed" does not add nearly as much value as "It is really important that everyone be present for our morning status meeting because that helps the team better coordinate efforts and share knowledge. Could we maybe try starting it thirty minutes later so that everyone is better able to attend?" In that scenario, your boss may ask follow up questions that lead to a discussion about Karen regularly missing the meeting, but they know that you approached the situation with a desire for process improvement rather than out of a personal vendetta.
- **Prepare specific examples.** Over the course of a day, managers hear a lot of people complain about a lot of things. The ratio of valid to invalid complaints varies from place to place, but there is a real risk of information overload. One way that you can differentiate your input is to provide specific examples of what harm is being caused by the issue you have identified. Expanding on the previous scenario about someone regularly missing the morning meeting, you should also provide some concrete instances of where it has caused problems. You might tell your boss "It is important that everyone be present for our morning status meetings, because it helps us work more efficiently. Just last week we had decided in that meeting to use

SQL only accounts for our project rather than full AD logins, but because not everyone was there, the AD logins were still requested, and we wasted a lot of time creating things we didn't need while also not getting the things we did need." If you can identify why a problem needs to be solved, then that helps your manager know that you are not just venting.
- **Give options.** Though this does not apply to every situation, I often like to provide options when discussing a problem with my manager. This invites them to be part of the conversation rather than simply telling them that I want a solution I have already picked. There are almost always multiple ways to solve a problem, and presenting options shows that you have thought through the issue and are really invested in solving it in a way that is beneficial to everyone and not just yourself.
- **Ask for help.** Sometimes you may have already tried everything you can think of to solve a problem on your own. I have definitely run into many issues that I wore myself out trying to fix with no success. Something that has worked well for me in this scenario is to ask my manager to help me figure out what I can do to better address the issue rather than asking them to fix the problem. Try to frame the conversation with something like this: "I cannot seem to get our team working efficiently with the database administrators. Over the past couple of months, I have started including them in our project planning meetings so that we don't take them by surprise with our requests. I have also met with one of them to try and define a mutually beneficial request process so that they have everything they need to start working as soon as we submit a request. However, the average turnaround time on things we ask them for is still over a week. Do you have any ideas for something else I could try to help improve our relationship with them?" This leads to a much more productive discussion than opening with "I'm sooooo sick of the database team. They're too slow, and I'm tired of waiting on them all the time."

Putting it all together.
Everything discussed in this section is pretty conceptual and will necessarily look different depending on the details of your particular job. Hopefully you will be able to take these concepts and apply them in your day to day. Figure out what works best for both you and your supervisor, and do not be afraid to change things up if anything does not work the way you expect it to on the first try.

Overall, your manager is the one who has the most impact on your ratings, reviews, and rewards. The easier you make your supervisor's life, the more they will trust and reward you. By being organized with your communication and work, you can create an environment in which you are perceived as proactive, competent, and mature. Be open to coaching and take feedback gracefully. Stressful situations can be diffused, and you can turn issues into positive experience with how you handle them. You should also be on the lookout for issues that can be used as opportunities for improvement and then be proactive about proposing solutions to them.

3. Communicate

When I first entered the working world, I was horribly annoyed with the communication that was (or more often, was not) taking place. Emails were unclear, meetings were disorganized, and many people seemed to completely ignore one or more mediums of communication (phone, IM, or email). I simply could not understand how a large company could operate effectively with such inefficient transfers of information.

What I have noticed over time is that the difficulty with communicating effectively is an issue pretty much everywhere. People in general talk, write, and send way more information than is absorbed in a useful way. There are usually issues on both ends, and it can be terribly frustrating for everyone involved. Though I do not presume to know how to solve the larger societal issues at play, I have learned a number of techniques over the years that will help improve communication among you and your coworkers.

Many people are not effective communicators and have no desire to be. This is challenging because it limits how well a team can work together and also creates negative perceptions from outside the organization. Exemplary employees not only communicate well but can effectively coax communication from others who might not willingly give it. An earlier chapter was called "Get things done". Communicating effectively both inside and outside of your team is essential to accomplishing this goal.

Here are some specific steps you can take to communicate more effectively in your workplace:

Be the change.

Early in my career, I had an epiphany that has forever changed my approach to communication. I could complain all day about what other people were not doing, but that would not make me one bit more effective or change the situation in any way. What I could do, though, was to analyze what I found lacking about the communication I was receiving. By learning from that, I was able to improve in my own communications with others. The more frustrated I became with the emails I was receiving, the more meticulously I monitored my own output. You don't need to go to a seminar or take an extensive online training class to start getting better at communicating. One of the best ways to improve your own communication skills is to simply observe what others do and make adjustments based on what you seeing being effective or ineffective.

Help others.
The rest of the sections in this chapter will focus on things you should do in your emails (and in your documentation, presentations, and phone calls), but I feel like it is appropriate to start by taking a moment to address how to get communication out of others. It is tempting and easy to take on the mindset that it is not your job to accommodate others who are unprofessional or unfriendly or incompetent. Many people take that attitude, and those people are not as effective in the workplace as they could be. Like it or not, your effectiveness at work depends heavily on your ability to communicate with others. Even if it is wildly unfair, if you use someone else's bad habits or personality quirks as reasoning for your failure to get things done, you will develop the reputation of someone who makes excuses instead of someone who finds a way to make things happen.

Here are some tactics for dealing with people who you are having a hard time communicating with:

- **Figure out their preferred method of communication:** Different people respond to different methods of communication. Over the course of my career, I have encountered people who respond religiously to email but cannot be bothered to look at instant messages or answer a phone. I've also met people who will dodge a phone call but always answer instant messages immediately. Some people operate entirely through text message. If you can figure out someone's preferred method of communication and then use it, then that takes away at least one excuse for them to not respond. If you are not sure what someone prefers, then either ask or mimic whatever form they used to initiate communication with you.
- **Figure out the process:** Do your best to understand the proper process for requesting work from the other person, and then follow that process. If an employee's performance is based mostly on how

many IT tickets they resolve in a day, then their motivation to answer email requests is probably pretty low. Create the ticket and help them help you. Follow the process first, and then reach out to them if you need to provide additional information.
- **Schedule a meeting to discuss how you can improve communication:** There have been a number of times in the past when I have consistently had issues getting what I need from someone. In the workplace, burning bridges rarely works out well, so I always avoid contacting someone else's manager unless I really have to. What I have often done instead is schedule a meeting with the other person, explain that my team will need an increased amount of assistance from their team in the future, and then ask what we could do to give them what they need in order to help us most effectively. Then I document the process we agree on and make sure that I follow it when contacting them in the future. This takes away the excuse of not having what information they need to get the task done and also helps do a reset of the relationship on good terms.
- **Include outside sources:** If really needed, copy a project manager or product owner on your communications. Increased visibility typically increases responsiveness. Be careful, though. Some people can take this as a sign of aggression and that does not motivate them to help you. Where I have used this effectively in the past is when I know someone is out of the office and I am not sure who else on their team to work with. Rather than waiting for them to come back into the office, I will ask their supervisor who I should contact in the meantime.
- **Do not be afraid to ask your supervisor for assistance:** If you are following process and someone on another team is completely unresponsive to your requests, then ask your supervisor for ideas on what to do next. Your supervisor often has more information and influence than you do, so it cannot hurt to get their input. Be sure not to overuse this tactic, though. Supervisors are not babysitters, and you should only involve them when you're completely blocked.

Only type what is true.
Anything you put in writing (whether it be email, IM, or text message) is something that can be used against you in the future. When you are not around to defend it, your words can take on a life of their own. In the rest of this chapter, we will discuss ways to make your communications more clear and understandable, but first and foremost, you must only write what is true.

As soon as your communication is written or recorded, it becomes a (somewhat) permanent record that can be referenced entirely independently.

The more detail you can provide in your written communication, the better others will be able to understand the context when they reference it. Many people think of email or IMs as transitory messages that are as short lived and as informal as a breakroom conversation. As soon as you send something, however, it can be forwarded or read by many people beyond the original audience. Always include enough detail that your words cannot be taken out of context.

Real Life Example:

In my first job, I was the most junior person on the team and had very little vacation. At the end of the year when everyone else was taking time off, I worked on a personal project to simplify password changes for the software system that my team supported. There was a larger issues with how those passwords were being stored, but my project was not aimed at fixing that issue - it was merely to save time and eliminate issues caused by typos. Upon completion, I added some very thorough documentation to our team wiki about what my project did and (more importantly) did not accomplish. It reduced the amount of time and resources needed for annual password changes and reduced the chance of users being locked out accidentally during that process. It did not make our connection strings compliant with what the company's security team had defined as acceptable, and I made sure to document that clearly. A particular team lead asked me to claim that it had fixed our compliance issue, but I would not, and I made it a point to emphasize that in my documentation.

About a year after I left that group and had moved on to a new job with the same company, one of my former coworkers called and told me that the team lead had tried to tell the security team that I had claimed my project fixed their compliance issue and cited that as the reason why the team had not fixed it before their audit. The wiki page that I had written ended up saving my reputation and protecting me from the fallout of the failed audit.

I know that this example is probably not the type of situation you come across every day, but it is something that has stuck with me throughout my career, and I think it illustrates the larger point. There are many reasons to write documentation. There are many audiences for your written communications. Regardless of audience or motivation, though, always write what is true. Stand by your work and do not leave room for interpretation.

Provide all the information needed to understand the issue.
As discussed in the previous section, context is important for written communication. Once something leaves your email client or phone, it takes on a life of its own, and you never know who will be reading it or when. It is to your advantage to provide enough detail for someone reading your email to understand the context and take action on it immediately with no follow up.

As someone who is constantly working on multiple projects and who receives entirely too much email, I can attest that there are a million good reasons why someone might not read your email at the exact moment that you send it. The more time that goes by, the less clear the memory of the non-written pieces of the conversation becomes. You should always craft your written communications in such a way that your audience could read it at any time in the future and immediately have all of the context that they need to do what you are asking of them.

To accomplish this goal, pay attention to the following things:

- **Be specific:** Do not write things like "Please change the password on that functional account we discussed." Do write things like "Please change the password on functional account DOMAIN\account". Even if you have just discussed something in person, there is no guarantee that the person to whom you are writing will remember it when they open the email, that they will have understood completely what you meant during that conversation, or even that they will be the one performing the work. For work-related emails, do not be afraid to over-explain.
- **Give context:** Following up on the previous example, an ideal email would look more like "Please change the password on functional account DOMAIN\account" in Active Directory and send me the password so that I can update it in our documentation. This can be done during normal business hours." If you are not a technology person, then do not be intimidated by this example. The real takeaway is that you need to think of any questions that you would have if someone sent you the email with no context, and then fill in that context so that there is no question about what you mean.

Something that I found wildly frustrating early in my career was the tendency that many people have to request something from me without giving me the information needed to complete the request. If your company operates with a ticketing system, then I am sure that you have shared this frustration when receiving tickets that are not specific or do not have enough context. This means that when you try to work on the ticket, you are unable to complete the request until the requestor is available for a follow up conversation. A tendency I have seen over and over again is that people tend to prioritize the work for which they have all the information needed. Do not give anyone an excuse to de-prioritize your work.

Do not write as if you are the audience.
Since we all live inside our own heads, it is very easy to write from that

perspective. The quickest way to write an email is to transcribe your own inner monologue onto the screen. It is a safe bet that most of your written communications contain all the information that you would need to take action or answer a question. The issue with this is that most people are not you. Whether you realize it or not, you have knowledge, connotations, and experience that others do not. If your written communication relies on that, then there is a very good chance that it will be misunderstood or ineffective.

An important part of communicating effectively is to know your audience and phrase your ideas in a way that they can grasp. Using technical jargon or talking about something extremely specific in your area of expertise can get in the way of this if your intended audience does not have the same level of understanding. Make sure that your written communications are at an appropriate level of detail for the recipient. An email to one of your team members and an email to your project manager should contain totally different levels of technical detail.

Copy everyone who needs to know.
One of the best things about email and text messages is that in the modern world they are basically free. There is no additional cost (and very little effort involved) for adding additional recipients to your emails. This can be a blessing and a curse.

The downfall of this technology is that we all get a lot of emails. Over the course of a week, it is easy to become numb to the constant onslaught of new items in your inbox. When I am in the middle of trying to figure out a problem, the last thing I need is the distraction of an email notification about something completely unrelated to my day to day. If someone constantly copies me on things that are irrelevant, then I tend to stop paying attention.

I can only assume that other people do the same, so I tend to be very deliberate about who I copy. If someone has specifically requested an update on something or expressed interest in an issue, then I might copy them on future communications. If I know of something that I think someone needs to be aware of for a larger reason, then often times I will copy them and then have a follow up conversation immediately after. Make all of your emails count, and people will be more likely to pay attention to them.

Be professional.
This should go without saying, but I have seen enough examples of the contrary that I wanted to take some time to emphasize it. Any time you engage in written communication in the workplace, it is tremendously important to be professional. Your work chat client is not your personal social

media feed. Your work emails are not private. Anything and everything that goes on within your company network is owned by the company and can be read by someone beyond your intended audience at any time.

I am definitely not saying that you cannot lightheartedly joke with coworkers or ask someone in another department how their kids are doing. Having work appropriate personal conversations is totally normal and fine. The important distinction you need to make is that at work you do not own your communication tools, which means that many people outside your intended audience may read your words. You do not want to write anything that could come across as unprofessional.

Name calling, personal attacks, inappropriate images, swearing, risqué humor, and stereotypes based on protected classes are all things that could get your fired or significantly set back your career. Do not derail yourself by being juvenile. When you are in the office, the communication tools provided to you by the company are for company communication. They own it. Treat it that way.

Let everyone know where you are.
Aside from the general advice about clear communication, there is one final point I would like to make regarding a specific type of information that should always be made available to all interested parties. No one you work with should ever need something from you and not have any idea where you are. There should never be a situation where your manager cannot answer an inquiry about whether or not you are in the office. There should never be a time when you miss a meeting and no one in the meeting knows in advance that you will not be there. There should never be a time when someone expects something from you but does not receive it and has no idea where you are or how to contact you.

Much like the previous point about being professional, this should go without saying, but I have seen it happen enough that I thought it was worth calling out explicitly. Few things create a more negative perception of someone than not knowing when you can expect them to actually show up or be available. Most places where I have worked in the past have treated employees like grownups. As long as you are willing to be available when something important is happening, then it is not problem if you occasionally need to leave early to pick up a relative from the airport or step out to meet the cable guy in the middle of the afternoon. You are allowed to manage your time as long as you do it responsibly. The quickest way to lose that privilege is to abuse it.

You do not need to share intimate details of your personal life with your manager or coworkers, but you do need to keep them up to date on your availability because it directly affects them. Your team most likely has a shared calendar of some sort where people can document when they will be out of the office. Make sure you keep that updated. If something out of the ordinary comes up on short notice, then call or text your manager and anyone else who will be impacted. If your team has a preferred messaging system, then use that. Whatever the means, make sure no one is surprised when you are not at your desk or in a meeting that you were supposed to attend.

Keep a level head.
It is great to have people on your team who are passionate about what they do. Employees who care about the quality of their work are a great asset for a company. This passion and enthusiasm, however, can occasionally manifest in the form of rather heated discussions. Also, some people just have short fuses or are dealing with things in their personal lives that can bleed over into their work performance. Whatever the reason, you may routinely find yourself in a discussion at work that crosses the line from professional discussion into emotional argument.

When a discussion gets heated, it is very natural to match the tone (especially when discussing something about which you have a strong opinion). Keep in mind, though, that you and your coworkers should be working toward a common goal and that at the end of the day the path forward that is best for the company is the one that should be chosen. It should never be "my idea vs your idea" but rather "let's choose the path forward is the best for our organization".

While you may not have a problem keeping a level head during these discussions, that does not mean that others will, so here are some approaches you can try when dealing with a discussion that has gotten out of hand:

- **Do not escalate.** When someone raises their voice or starts insulting others or just generally begins being unprofessional in a discussion, things can begin to devolve very quickly if others join in and do the same. No matter what your coworkers are doing, do not raise your voice. Do not be petty or passive aggressive. Keep it about ideas and not about individuals. You cannot control others, but you can control yourself. Your manager will notice this.
- **Hear the argument and repeat it back.** When someone is heated, they are not communicating effectively. There may be a long rant that is interwoven with current gripes, past grievances, personal attacks,

and many other topics that have no bearing on the current decision. Do your best to look past all this and only respond to the concerns that are relevant to the task at hand. Repeat back to them your understanding of their issue and then ask for confirmation or clarification. In my experience, a lot of times when someone gets heated, it is because they feel like they are not being heard or their concerns are not being taken seriously. Oftentimes if someone feels like their side of the argument is being understood and addressed, then they are more likely to de-escalate and re-engage in productive discussion.

- **Call a timeout.** Sometimes when things have taken a negative turn, the best course of action is to shut down the discussion entirely. Try saying something along the lines of "I feel like we're at a bit of a stalemate here. I, personally, think that I could contribute more effectively to this discussion if I had some time to look into a few things. Could we maybe break for now and resume this afternoon or tomorrow?" This approach gives everyone a chance to walk away from the situation, calm down, and then think about how to move forward in a less emotionally charged way.
- **Bridge the gap.** If you have team members who are at the point where they are not able to effectively talk to each other, then try to help repair the relationship. Something I have done in the past is to go to each of them, try to get an understanding of their position and concerns, and then summarize it all in writing. Then I document the problem that needs to be solved, the proposed solutions, and the outstanding concerns, and that becomes the agenda for the next meeting. This approach has often helped focus the discussion and also helped everyone see that they already agree on more than they previously realized.

Improve if you need to.

Not everyone is a gifted communicator, but everyone can be an effective communicator. If you struggle with grammar, spelling, or even with summarizing your thoughts in such a way that they are meaningful to others, then you are not doomed. By taking advantage of a few helpful resources and putting in just a little bit of effort, you can easily improve your communication.

One of the biggest barriers to improving your communication is acknowledging that you are not doing it effectively. Others will rarely call you out for poor communication. Instead, you will routinely see the consequences: arguments, wasted time, misaligned expectations, misunderstanding, and poor working relationships with others. If you are feeling frustrations in any of these areas, then it is worth your while to re-examine your communication methods and style to see if they are contributing to the issues.

Aside from the other points already made in this chapter, here are some additional resources that you can use to help your written communications:

- **Get a proofreader.** Any time I am going to send an email to more than five people or to someone more than two rungs higher than me on the org chart, I get someone else to proofread it first. This is helpful for catching grammar or spelling errors, but it also is a good way to make sure that what you have written is cohesive and makes sense to an outside party. It can also be very helpful to get a proofreader who knows the people in your intended audience better than you do. This way they can give an insider's perspective on how effectively you have communicated what the recipients want to know.
- **Use online tools.** There are plenty of free tools online to help with spelling, punctuation, and grammar. My wife swears by Grammarly. Most email clients have a decent spellchecker built in, but I still routinely paste things into Microsoft Word before sending.
- **Find a good template.** It is very easy to hit reply on an email and then immediately brain dump a response and hit send. Many email clients will allow you to create a default template for email responses. Try creating one with a salutation, a few short paragraphs of example text, and a signature. This will help you stay in the mindset of structuring your outgoing communications deliberately.

Putting it all together.
Everything discussed in this section is pretty universal in the world of digital communication. Hopefully you will be able to take these concepts and apply them in your day to day. Figure out what works best in your environment, and do not be afraid to change things up if anything does not work the way you expect it to on the first try.

Communication is an essential part of your ability to work effectively. When you have trouble communicating with someone else, then figure out a way to improve it. Be sure to provide enough context that your audience can understand what you are saying or asking. Make sure that everyone who needs the information receives it. Think about your written communication from the perspective of those who will be reading it, and always be professional and truthful. Be courteous and make sure that people can find you when they need you. Do not add fuel to the fire when discussions get heated. Finally, if you are not a gifted communicator, then acknowledge it and take steps to improve.

YOUR CAREER SUCKS

4. Follow Through

A distinguishing characteristic of exemplary employees is that they appreciate the importance of and facilitate the accomplishment of larger organizational goals. A big part of this is follow through. Most people are good about saying they will do the right things. Few people are good at consistently doing them. Whether it is a request from your boss, one of your team members, or someone from another group, following through and actually doing the things you commit to in a timely manner goes a long way and will not go unnoticed.

As I have mentioned several times already, there are a lot of things in any large organization that can be terribly frustrating. My response has typically been to pay attention, figure out what it is that someone else is doing that I find difficult to deal with, and then to be very conscious of not doing that to others. A good example that falls into this category is when someone says they will do something and then does not.

Over the course of a normal day, many things will happen that can distract you from commitments. It is very easy to tell someone that you will get back to them after a meeting and then go back to your desk to find a slew of unread emails, messages, and voicemails. You go into firefighter mode and whatever happened in the previous meeting starts to fade away. This is completely and totally normal and understandable, but that also makes it a prime area in which to distinguish yourself.

As you begin to be known as the type of person who can be relied upon to get things done, you will find that more people come to you first when they need something. This is great for your career and makes your strong work ethic visible to more people. You do not have to be the smartest or the most experienced person on your team to have the best skills in follow through, so focus on developing that as you grow your other talents.

Here are some easy ways that you can develop a reputation as someone with follow through:

If you say you'll do something, then do it.
As already discussed, being the type of person who can be relied upon to deliver what they say they will deliver is something that will set you apart from your peers. A key part of doing this successfully, though, is knowing your limits and setting realistic expectations.

Something I have noticed over time is that many people feel pressure to "go with the flow" in meetings and either commit to doing things they do not know how to do or not time box their commitments. There is absolutely no need for this, and doing it only sets you up for failure. Make sure that your communications are accurate and set expectations appropriately.

We all have more work on our plates than we have time to complete over the course of a day. Prioritization and coordination are essential parts of organizational success. This cannot be done well without accurate information. In the heat of the moment, it is easy to over promise, but do not give in to that temptation. What I have generally found to be true is that people are much more willing to forgive lack of experience than lack of planning.

Consider the following scenarios:

Scenario 1:
You are in a meeting for a project with a tight deadline. Another team is waiting for your team to set up a new functional account for them so that they can configure a testing environment. You are new to the team and have no idea how to set up a functional account or the level of effort involved. When asked if you can have it done by Wednesday, you say yes, and everyone seems pleased. By Wednesday, you realize that the process is more complicated than you thought and you do not have all the information needed to set up the account. You show up to the Wednesday project meeting and tell everyone that you were not able to get the account created. At the end of the day on Thursday, you finally deliver the account to the team that needs it.

Scenario 2:
You are in a meeting for a project with a tight deadline. Another team is waiting for you team to set up a new functional account for them so that they can configure a testing environment. You are new to the team and have no idea how to set up a functional account or the level of effort involved. When asked if you can have it done by Wednesday, you say

that you have not previously set up that type of account but that you can look into it with your team and let everyone know a timeline by the end of the day. After the meeting, you follow up with a team member and realize that the process is more complicated than you thought and that you do not have all the information needed to set up the account. You email all of the project stakeholders and let them know that there is a little more pre-work to be done but that the account should be ready by Friday at the latest. You end up having it set up and ready by the end of the day Thursday.

Even though the timelines are exactly the same in both scenarios, the efficiency of the project team and their perception of you is significantly different.

In Scenario 1, everyone leaves the Wednesday meeting thinking of you as someone who does not hit deadlines. The team waiting on the account may have prioritized a lot of work with the expectation of having it on Wednesday, and that may have come at the expense of other project tasks or organizational initiatives. Even though the deliverable was only a day late, the perception hit is not insignificant. Any goodwill that you may have accumulated by agreeing to the unrealistic date initially will have been wiped away.

In Scenario 2, however, everyone leaves the Wednesday meeting feeling like things are on track. The fact that you did the investigation and followed up quickly leaves everyone with the impression that you feel a sense of ownership for the project and will do what it takes to get it done in a timely manner despite your inexperience. This is a great reputation to have. Setting an achievable goal of Friday sets you up to deliver on time (or early) and allows everyone to plan accordingly. The project team walks away with the perception that while you are still learning the job, you have a strong sense of maturity and follow through.

Do not be a Yes Man (or Yes Woman). In the long run, anyone would much rather have an accurate idea of when they can expect something than to be told what they want to hear but with no follow through. You may not be able to give someone an answer they want immediately, but if you give them enough information that they can plan realistically, then it helps move things forward for others as well as yourself.

Give accurate updates.
Aside from setting expectations accurately, it is also very important to give accurate updates for the things you are working on - especially if they are taking longer than expected. We all get into situations where we are working on something that ends up being a lot more complicated than anticipated at

the outset. A lot of people tend to default toward a status update of "I'm working on it" and then hoping desperately that no one asks a follow up question. Exemplary employees do not do that.

Running into problems or unforeseen additional complexity is not a sign of weakness. For some people it may be hard to admit when something is hard for them, but you need to keep in mind that what you are working on probably affects other people. Even if a project manager is not happy with how long a task is taking, they would always rather know about the issue sooner rather than later. If your coworkers are operating on a timeline and going above and beyond and working overtime to hit a deadline that is no longer accurate because of something only you know, then you are not being a good team player.

As a general principle, I like to be as transparent as possible about what I am working on and how it is progressing. My experience has been that if I ever do not feel comfortable letting everyone know exactly what I am working on and where I am on it, then there are larger issues that need to be addressed. Stay aligned with the priorities set by your manager or project manager, communicate frequently and accurately, and make sure that the people working with you know when there is a delay.

Write it down, check it off.
As already mentioned, it is tremendously easy to get distracted over the course of your day. If your work environment is anything like any of the ones I have been in, then you are constantly bombarded by emails, instant messages, phone calls, people stopping by your desk, and things from your personal life that have to be done during normal working hours. It is almost the exception to NOT be distracted by something pressing between the time you leave a meeting or have a conversation and when you get back to your desk. One method that I have found to be effective in spite of these challenges is to simply write things down.

When I write something down, I am a million times more likely to remember details of it than if I simply talk about it or even type it. Something about the act of thinking about it and using letters to capture it makes it stick better in my brain. I think that writing something down also signals to everyone else in a meeting or conversation that I am serious about what I say I am going to do. This is what works for me. Find something that works for you, and then do it regularly.

Another important concept is to hold yourself accountable to the things your write down (or type or make voice memos about or whatever). At a previous place of employment, I had a notebook, and every day I would draw a horizontal line. I would write the date under the line and then any time I committed to doing something throughout the day, I would write it down and put a star by it. At the end of the day, I would not go home until I had crossed out all my stars as complete. Now I tend to work more in Post-Its or note cards. Sometimes by the end of the day, my brain is dead, and I need a break. I will go home, exercise, eat dinner with my wife, and then log back in and pull the note card out of my wallet and finish off anything remaining. I rarely go to bed before completing and throwing away my note card. This is an easy way of enforcing a not so easy habit.

You cannot control other people, but you should control yourself.
In addition to getting distracted, another big enemy of follow through is the temptation to let someone else's lack of it affect your own. I cannot count the number of times in the past that I have been in a meeting where someone says that they need to follow up with me after, and then they simply never do it. If a task is associated with you or you have been identified as a dependency, then make sure that you do everything you can to get it done. Sometimes that means reaching out to someone who should be reaching out to you.

Consider a scenario where you are in a meeting with several people and everyone leaves with an action item. A coworker from the server team is supposed to send you login credentials for a new server by the end of the day. When you get those credentials, you are supposed to configure the server to host your application by the end of the week. Another coworker from the security team is supposed to contact you to conduct a security audit of the new server once it has been configured. By noon the next day, you have not heard anything from either of them.

Thought it would be easy to sit at your desk and keep yourself busy with other tasks, an exemplary employee would find a way to move things forward. Even though the coworker from the server team was supposed to contact you, it would be much more effective to be proactive and reach out. People routinely get busy and either forget to close out a task (in this case by notifying you that the server is ready) or neglect to keep other people informed when something is taking longer than expected. If the server is going to be delayed, then that would be a good thing to find out early on so that you can begin notifying others that your task may not be completed by the originally agreed upon deadline. If the server is ready, then you can begin working.

Even though it would not directly impact your ability to deliver on time, I would also recommend reaching out to your coworker from the security team to at least schedule a time to get together to work on the security audit. If the server is going to be delayed, then you can at least have the security assessment done by the original deadline. Missing a deadline is easier to sell when you can report that you did not complete one task due to external factors but that you did complete all of the others. It is also a good way to support the security team and help head off anything that could slow down your project later on.

A huge key to functioning as an exemplary employee is to simply get stuff done. Doing that for you is one thing, but finding ways to do it for larger groups (a project team, your team of immediate coworkers, etc.) is an even bigger challenge. Individual recognition may not come overnight, but if you are the type of person who adds an increased amount of reliability and follow through to your teams, then that will not go unnoticed. Many people find ways to be productive on their own. A next level quality that will set you apart is to consistently add spread that mindset to those who are working on the same larger-scale goals as you.

Putting it all together.
Everything discussed in this section is pretty universal in the working world. Hopefully you will be able to take these concepts and apply them in your day to day. Figure out what works best in your environment, and do not be afraid to change things up if anything does not work the way you expect it to on the first try.

Follow through is a quality that easy in concept but hard in execution. One of the most important things you can do is learn to have follow through consistently - not just when you think you are in the spotlight. Most people have a strong sense of follow through on project tasks or assignments from their supervisor. Truly exceptional employees do it regardless of audience. Come up with a system that helps you hold yourself accountable and start developing the reputation of someone who can always be relied upon to deliver when they say they will deliver.

5. Take Goals Seriously

An important part of success within an organization is being able to understand what that organization values. While it is important to do work that you find meaningful and to walk away with a sense of personal accomplishment at the end of the day, it is also important to push forward organizational priorities if you want to experience long term career success. There are almost always things that the organization values that exist completely outside your day to day tasks. Keeping an eye out for opportunities to participate in these things is never a bad move.

One area that I regularly see hard workers completely neglect is the performance review process. Since goals and results are not directly related to accomplishing work tasks, they tend to seem less important. Since not doing these things well will not put your job in jeopardy, it is easy to move them down the priority list as more pressing assignments arrive. The truth is that while the performance review process may not seem like a big deal or may not appear to have negative consequences when you don't give it your full effort, your goals and results can actually play a huge role in how your organization views you.

The review process is something that is meant to be codified and consistent across the company. When it comes time for raises and bonuses, there is only so much money to go around, and your performance review is your resume when applying for a raise. Make sure that what you write is aligned with the things the company values, and make sure you effectively communicate how the work you did over the course of the year supported them.

Set meaningful performance goals.
If I had seventy-five cents for every time I heard someone say something

disparaging about goals/results/performance reviews, then I could have retired a long time ago. I cannot say that I do not get where people are coming from. Writing performance goals does not help you hit project deadlines or allow you to leave work on time or leave you with a particular sense of accomplishment. I am not going to argue that the goal setting process is fun or rewarding or even interesting. I will, however, argue that it is one hundred percent worth your time.

Hear me out. From my perspective, performance evaluations are the method by which your company allows you to communicate the value you add as an employee to the people who make decisions about compensation. Setting goals means setting the tone of that conversation. If you want a raise and you are not giving serious consideration to your performance goals and results, then you cannot blame anyone but yourself for your lack of success.

When you work on your annual performance goals, you should be setting yourself up to make a case for your own value. Whether you want a raise, a new position, additional responsibilities, or a bonus, your goals are the first step to proving you deserve it. Most companies have a published (internally) list of criteria for salary grades or titles or whatever categorization they give to different levels of salary and responsibility. This list typically contains a very detailed description of everything that is expected of employees who are in that level. This can be a great starting point for writing your goals. If you know exactly what the expectations are of someone in the salary grade you desire, then why would you not write all your goals in those terms?

Good goal setting will always involve a conversation with someone more senior than yourself. This could be your supervisor, your HR rep, or a mentor. Tell them what you want to work toward and then ask them what they see as the key areas in which you need to improve in order to get there. Using your company's list of salary grade expectations to frame this discussion can be especially helpful.

If you want to stretch yourself in the coming year to earn a promotion, then go through the list ahead of time and take an honest assessment of yourself. Identify the areas in which you need to improve, and then have a follow up discussion with your supervisor about opportunities that he or she might suggest for developing yourself in those areas. Make it a collaborative process and take feedback gracefully. Your supervisor is often your biggest ally in working toward a promotion, so make sure that you are partnering toward a common goal.

If you feel that you have already earned a promotion but have not received it yet, then use your company's list of expectations as a starting point for creating some documentation. Show up to your goals discussion with your supervisor with a list of specific examples of how you feel you satisfy the criteria for each requirement. State calmly that getting to the next salary grade is important to you and that you feel you are currently satisfying all the requirements. Ask your supervisor where he or she sees gaps and ask for suggestions for improvement. This will help you target your goals more specifically to getting you where you want to go. Also, if you feel like you are close, do not be afraid to add some of the skills from the next salary grade beyond the one you are trying to achieve. Never stop improving.

Something else that I have found to be particularly effective when setting goals is to tie them to larger team, organizational, or company goals or values. Companies invest a lot of time in setting their internal values and in planning company-wide initiatives. If you can tie your goals to these things, then that shows you understand the bigger picture beyond your day to day and are aligned with the direction of the company. If the company has an internal goal of moving as much as possible into a cloud hosted environment over the next year, then a great goal would be to do a POC of migrating one of your team's existing applications into the cloud. This aligns with the larger organizational goal and also gives you an opportunity to learn a new skill and help lead the team in that area.

Finally, take your goals seriously. Use them as a way to push yourself. If training is available that will benefit you in the long term, then include it in your goals. Use that as a way of holding yourself accountable for completing it. If you want to keep your career moving, then let your goals lead the way.

Write meaningful performance results.
The essential counterpart of each performance goal is a performance result. Your goals and results documentation should read like a series of persuasive essays. Each goal is a statement, and each result is a piece of evidence that supports that statement. The more examples you can give the better (as long as they are good examples).

Your performance results should have the following qualities:

- **Good results are specific.** Each of your results should tell a way in which you personally added value. Writing that you were part of a team that hit a deadline is not a good result. Explaining what you specifically did to help the team achieve that goal is what will make it a compelling argument.
- **Good results can be understood by a wide audience.** During the

performance evaluation process your goals and results will most likely be viewed by a wide variety of people from different backgrounds and with different levels of familiarity with your work. Avoid making your results so technical that their significance cannot be understood by a non-technical person. Anyone should be able to pick up your goals and results document and be able to understand what you accomplished.

- **Good results reinforce the goal with which they are associated.** While it is always good to provide context, you cannot assume that whoever is reading your goals and results will not also being reading everyone else's goals and results on the same day. Keep yours short and to the point, and make sure that everything in a result ties back to the goal that it is supporting. It is totally fine to reuse a single experience across multiple goals as long as you explain only the parts that are relevant to each goal.
- **Good results are phrased in terms of business value.** An A+ result is one that demonstrates that you have both achieved your goal AND done it in such a way that business value was provided. This shows that you understand the significance of your work and have found a way to align your personal goals with those of the organization.

Putting it all together.
I realize this chapter has been pretty high level. Every office has a different performance review process, and the details will vary from company to company. Hopefully the ideas discussed here can be easily applied to your own situation. As always, do not be afraid to change things up if anything does not work the way you expect it to on the first try.

Goals and results are a pain, but they are completely and totally worth the effort. If you use your company's list of salary grade expectations, base your goals on your desired level, deliver on those goals, and then use your results to reinforce that you are doing everything required of that level, then you should start seeing consistent career growth. If you are doing all of that and not seeing career advancement, then this is a sign of organizational instability, and you should consider looking at other companies that do a better job of honoring their own process.

Here are some final thoughts on mastering the goals/results process:

- **Keep notes throughout the year.** For me, it is very difficult to remember what I had for breakfast yesterday. Remembering the specifics of something I worked on eleven months ago is not going to happen unless I do some digging in old emails, notebooks, or project documents. Keeping a text document with some quick notes on major projects that I work on is an easy way to speed up the process of writing results at the end of the year. Weekly highlights are a good way of doing this as well. If you are writing weekly highlights anyway, then keep them all together in a text file for future reference.

- **Goals and results are valuable enough to write on your own time.** A fundamental flaw that I have observed over and over is that people often adopt the mindset of "If I'm not given time to work on my goals in the office, then I'm not going to write them." The misconception here is the idea that goals are something you are doing for the company. In reality, goals are something you should be doing for you. You are the one who can benefit from it. I have never been given dedicated time to work on my goals at work. I have always worked on them at home. I consider this a worthwhile investment of time.
- **Get your goals done early and review them with someone more senior than yourself before submitting.** Writing good goals and results is a time consuming process. Make time for it long enough before the deadline for submission that you can review with your supervisor/HR rep/mentor or whoever is giving you career guidance. The intended audience for your documentation is not yourself, so it is worth getting someone else's input before formally submitting it.
- **Make sure your performance results tell the whole story.** If you help out with company event planning, attend training, represent your company at a career fair, mentor an intern, or otherwise do things that benefit the company outside your normal day to day responsibilities, then you should absolutely include those things in your results.

6. LEAVE THE ROLE BETTER THAN YOU FOUND IT

Every job you are hired to do will have a key set of responsibilities associated with it. When budget is allocated for a position, there is usually a specific need or pain point associated with it. When you start, make sure you learn those key responsibilities and quickly get to the point where you can perform them well. To reiterate an earlier point, become competent as quickly as possible.

While you are getting up to speed, though, you will probably notice a lot of things about the strengths and weaknesses of the organization that you have joined. Again, the best way to contribute immediately is simply to do the job you were hired to do. There would never have been approval to hire someone if there was not a specific need. Focus on learning what you need to learn to do the job as quickly as possible. Do not stop there, however. I always get nervous if I feel like I am doing the same thing every day. The working world is a dynamic one. Make sure that you are doing things that provide value and not just things that you are comfortable with.

Team needs will shift and change over time. As people leave, roll off on project assignments, or simply get tired of doing the same thing every day, there will be new skill gaps that need to be filled. In any workplace you will probably encounter some people who spend a lot of time explaining why they cannot take on any more responsibilities and other people who always seem to be willing to jump in and learn something new. Exemplary employees can identify team needs and take steps to address them. Be the type of person who fills gaps.

You should also always be looking for opportunities for process improvement. When something seems disorganized or overly stressful, there is probably a way to make it better. Many times people get in the habit of doing things one way, and a fresh set of eyes can provide valuable insight about potential opportunities for change that would benefit everyone. Certainly do not start a new job by walking around informing everyone that they are doing things incorrectly, but do pay attention to pain points and see if you can learn more about why things are being done the way they are. Tactfully suggest improvements when the time is right or volunteer to take ownership of the process so that you can experiment with adjusting it.

One word of caution to go along with this chapter. There is a big difference between expanding your role and overextending yourself. While it is good to volunteer and learn new things, you should use good judgement and not overcommit. A lot of chapters in this book talk about ways to make sure your manager knows what you are doing and working on. Let your boss help you balance your workload and make sure that you understand priorities.

Here are some ways that you can make your role more valuable to your team/organization:

Volunteer.
An easy way to increase the value you contribute to your team is to simply volunteer when no one else will. I have been in so many meetings where someone identifies a team need and everyone in the room looks down and tries to appear busy. Most managers I have worked with would much prefer having someone volunteer for an opportunity than having to assign it to someone. It is to your advantage to be known as the type of person who has a good attitude and is not afraid to try something new.

Some of my greatest career successes have come from volunteering to learn things that no one else wanted to work on. It has been my experience that people on any team are much more willing to share knowledge with you if they perceive that you are making an honest effort to learn how to do something that they do not enjoy. If I hate changing database passwords, then I will probably be very willing to teach someone else to do it and then no longer have it on my plate. Changing passwords is not sexy work, but if you are new to a team and do not have a lot of experience yet, then volunteering to take it on could be very beneficial. It is something you can get up to speed on quickly, and it frees up other team members to do more interesting things. It also expands your role and helps you take ownership of a process.

To be clear, the goal is not to own a bunch of processes. If you spend all day on boring password changes and routine maintenance, then you will not have a lot of time left over to learn new things or continue to expand your role. When you take over a troublesome process, your goal should be to make it so quick and easy that anyone can do it. Automate it if you can. Then it becomes a process that the team owns and is not tied to any one individual. Many times the only reason one person has to perform a particular task every time is simply because no one else has taken the time to ask how to do it.

Create documentation.
A key part of doing something successfully is implementing enough documentation that other people can quickly get up to speed on it without talking to you directly. Simplifying a process does not help anyone unless they know how to implement it. You never want to be the single point of failure for anything. Clear, thorough documentation is a good way to prevent that.

Even if no one else seems interested in what you are learning or working on, it is a great idea to create documentation for it on a team wiki or shared drive. One advantage of this is that you will not forget. If you are learning a process that only needs to be done once per quarter, then you can save a lot of time by taking all the mystery out of it for your future self. Documentation takes time initially, but the earlier you do it, the sooner you start reaping the benefit.

Documentation is also a great way of starting a conversation among team members. A lot of times, if you ask your team members what a process should be, they will respond either with complete ambivalence or get lost on tangential conversations that does not actually advance the cause of clarifying the topic at hand. Creating a document that explains how you think a process is defined and asking for feedback helps focus the conversation. It is also a good test of how well you have absorbed the information. Openly and enthusiastically encourage feedback and integrate it quickly when you receive it. "Actually writing it down" seems to derail a lot of people when it comes to sharing knowledge. Take away the hurdle, and things can move very quickly.

Finally, documentation is an easy way to demonstrate the value you add. As already discussed, performance goals and results are an important part of your career. One way that you can reinforce your results is to add links to documentation you have created. For example, if you created a bunch of employee onboarding documentation, then you might write about it in your results and also provide the link to your training materials. If you improved a process, then put that in your results and link to the wiki page or document where you outlined it.

Facilitate healthy discussion.
The true strength of a team in not realized unless the individual members of that team are working together. Simply working close to a few other people does not make you a team any more than sitting next to some musicians on a

bus makes you part of a band. A good team approaches every issue with a variety of diverse experiences and perspectives. You could spend a week writing a document about a process you were learning, but that document would probably be much less valuable than if a couple of more senior members of the team worked on it together for an hour. In those types of situations, you may not be able to provide the technical expertise, but you can absolutely provide the organization and willingness to capture the thoughts on (digital) paper.

Getting buy in and consensus is an important part of contributing to your team's success. You never want to operate in a vacuum. There are no easy answers on how to do this effectively, but you can feel it out and see what works and what does not. From my own experience, asking humbly for input, taking good notes, and then documenting what you learn accurately is a good way to start. Over time, if your coworkers see you as someone who makes their lives easier, then they will be more willing to buy into your suggestions. This is a good feedback loop that will help strengthen the team while also expanding your role.

Putting it all together.
Every job is different, and what is needed from you in the short term varies. There will, however, always be opportunities to increase the value that your role provides over time. Look for chances to improve existing processes, to document or automate recurring tasks, and to facilitate discussion among team members on ways to improve things. The first draft of anything is never perfect, so do not be afraid to change things up over time.

Never stop looking for things to fix. Focus on what is in your sphere of influence. When you are involved with a bad process, then work with your team to fix it, document the solution, and make sure everyone understands the documentation. High performers strengthen the teams that they join, and in doing that they learn more about the work and expand their influence. No matter how mundane a job may seem from the start, never stop looking for ways to expand your role and work on things that are valuable.

This chapter has been very conceptual so far, so here are a couple of specific examples of putting it all into practice.

Real Life Example:

One summer during an internship, there were some unforeseen complications that kept me from being able to work on one of the projects that had been set aside for me. Rather than browsing the internet all day, I asked my technical mentor if I could spend some time job shadowing him. We talked about a lot of his day to day tasks, and eventually he suggested that I might take on his weekly report generation responsibilities for the summer. I sat with him, learned and documented the process, and then spent most of the rest of my free time that summer automating the process so that he would not have to spend so much time on it in the future. He was very pleased, and I received a full time job offer before I even went back to campus.

Real Life Example:

Shortly after beginning a junior level developer position, a very large project was undertaken that required a massive amount of work from the whole team. A big piece of it involved working in an outdated scripting language that had to be edited with a tool that was generally a huge pain and had a high learning curve. A senior member of the team was the expert in that particular technology, and I could see the pain in his eyes anytime anyone brought up the pending work for the project. One day after a planning meeting, I walked by his desk and asked if he would be willing to teach me how to update those scripts. Even though he was super busy, he took the time to sit down with me and walk through it. I took furious notes. Afterwards, I went back to my desk and documented the entire process (with screenshots). I was able to contribute significantly on the project, and I had a great relationship with that senior team member from that day until I left the group to pursue another opportunity years later.

Real Life Example:

In another role, there was a custom piece of software that we worked on that involved a heavy dependency on a third party library. Before go-live, I worked with the project stakeholders to establish a clearly defined process for library upgrades. Due to the nature of the work and the library, the timing of the upgrades had to be closely monitored and coordinated by our compliance team. At the end of the project, in addition to handing them a working piece of software, I also handed them documentation on how to request updates. On my team's internal wiki, I had a step by step guide for completing and testing the update process. The first time an update was requested, I paired with another team member while they followed the documentation and performed the change. After that anyone on the team was just as capable as anyone else of performing that update, and no one had to call me if an update needed to happen while I was on vacation.

7. Never Stop Making Yourself More Valuable

At the beginning of this book, we discussed competency. For any job, there will be a specific set of tasks or responsibilities for which you are responsible. Getting up to speed quickly is essential. Equally essential, though, is continuing to make yourself more valuable over time. This is important both for your career within the company and for your future.

In the chapter about competency, I mentioned that staying competent is important. One of my goals for this book is to be as pragmatic as possible. Something as open ended as "stay up to speed" is too vague to take action on, so I would like to revisit that. We all only have so much time in a day, and learning how to spend that time effectively while still having capacity for the other things you enjoy in life is an important skill.

One way of balancing this is to set aside a certain amount of time each week for learning something new. Maybe it is the first two hours of your day on Friday, or maybe it is the last hour of your day on Thursday. What is reasonable for you will probably depend on a lot of factors, but the point is to make sure you set aside time each week to learn and then stick to it. Block time on your calendar and go to a conference room or develop a habit of going to the library for an hour after work one night a week if you need to eliminate distractions. Reserve a reasonable amount of time for learning and then protect it.

I think there can be a clear distinction between increasing your internal value at a company and increasing your external value outside that company. Many times they can overlap - if you are learning a new skill for your job that is also in high demand externally, then you are increasing your value internally and externally. The reason I think of them separately, though, is that I think it provides good perspective on how to manage your learning time.

Investing time in increasing your internal value is obviously something your company will get behind. You should be doing it to some extent every day. For your long term success, though, I would highly encourage you to dedicate time to experiment and play. If you write C# code all day, then spend some time learning more about C# and the tools available for it. There are always ways to get better at what you do. If you ever think you have "arrived" in a particular skill, then you have really just become complacent.

Making sure that you are also increasing your external value is something that you may have to be more deliberate about. With any job, there is a danger of going heads down and becoming so specialized that you are no longer marketable externally. It is also easy to fall prey to group think, which is not good for you or your team. If your company uses Angular 1 and you become a master of it, then your company will probably be quite pleased. If you ever need to find a job externally, though, and realize that the rest of the world is using Angular 4, then you have done yourself a disservice. There are also reasons the rest of the world is no longer using Angular 1. Investing time in learning what others in your industry are doing is a benefit to both you personally and to your ability to contribute to your company. Your company may or may not give you assignments to investigate the outside world, though, so be sure that you periodically spend time getting up to speed.

Here are some more specific comments about how to increase both types of value:

Increase your internal value.
You have probably heard people say that day traders do not care if the stock market is up or down as long as it is moving. Change creates opportunity. I feel the same way about any job environment. I concede that my experience is probably a little exaggerated due to the nature of a career in technology, but I feel like every company changes a lot over time. People come and go, projects spin up and go away, budgets grow and shrink, and priorities constantly change. Some people hate change and do everything they can to oppose it. Exemplary employees see change as an opportunity to contribute more, learn something new, and take on new responsibilities. Priorities and needs will change. That is the nature of work. It is to your advantage to be attuned to this and to be prepared to get on board as quickly as possible.

A lot of people I have worked with in the past have been very resistant to change. Over time they begin to settle into a routine and are put off when there is a change in priorities or if they are asked to do something different. At the end of the day, your company writes your paycheck. That gives them the right to prioritize what you work on. Granted, in some cases a weakness in management might lead to misalignment with larger goals or a gross misprioritization of essential tasks, but that is a separate topic. In most cases, it is to your advantage to embrace change, keep a good attitude, and help things move forward.

You should work toward developing a reputation of being helpful at managing change. When a disruption to the normal swing of things occurs, do your best to get up to speed quickly and then help implement a transition plan. There tends to be a stark contrast between the way management sees an employee who is resistant to change and one who helps implement it. This is a skill set that is beyond just your specific job responsibilities, and it is something that will separate you from the average employee. Specific instances of helping manage change also make great examples to put in your end of year results.

Beyond changing priorities, there also tends to be a fair amount of change in needed skill sets for a particular team over time. Whether your company is taking on support for a new version of a vended application or offering a new service or transitioning to the cloud, there will often be things that someone needs to learn. These situations are again very good chances for you to learn something new that makes your more valuable to the organization. Many employees will shy away from new challenges, so this is yet another way to distinguish yourself.

Let's look at two specific philosophies that will help you continually increase your value within your organization:

- **Dig in.** It will take time to get fully up to speed on the skills needed for your job. Equally important, though is learning about everything your job impacts and is impacted by. A lot of people focus on expertise in the specific skill or task that they do on a daily basis. While this is great and definitely adds value, it can also lead to a very limited view of how things work and can limit your contribution when working with other teams or proposing solutions to larger issues. Your company can probably hire someone with experience in the basic skills needed to do your job pretty easily. What they cannot so easily hire is someone who has the broader organizational knowledge that is specific to their own environment.
  In a previous job, one approach that I found to work very well was to simply schedule a short meeting with one person from each of the teams that my team regularly interacted with. I would learn a little

more about what they did and then also ask what they would prefer from my team (at what point in the process do you want us to involve you in a project, how much lead time would you prefer for requests from our team, how should the requests be submitted, what types of information do you care about when we submit a work request, etc). This set us up to work more effectively with them in the future, but it also gave me a whole new appreciation for the company's overall organization and infrastructure. This knowledge helped me propose better solutions, prevent issues earlier in the process, and communicate and plan more effectively. Needless to say, those simple conversations made me significantly more valuable as an employee. Armed with this knowledge, you will also be more prepared to see where things are going and what opportunities are on the horizon. When you understand the big picture, you can begin to see how change cascades across the organization, and you can better prepare yourself for it. When you know a big proof of concept project is going on for a new technology on another team, it is a pretty safe bet that you may need to know something about that technology and how it impacts your team in the near future. Stay ahead of the game and position yourself to be ready to help embrace change rather than oppose it.

Every company is different, but if you are deliberate about it, you should not have any trouble finding easy ways to increase your internal value. Keep improving your skills, but also increase your organizational knowledge. Get outside of your immediate team and find out how it all works together. Keep an eye on the future, and always be ready for change.

- **Say yes.** One of the best ways to keep your internal value on the upswing is to simply say yes to opportunities. Sometimes this will apply to your supervisor asking for someone willing to take on a new task. Sometimes it will apply to your director asking if you would be interested in a different position within the company. The biggest steps in my career have come from saying yes to opportunities that a lot of other people would not have. You should also keep an open mind to changes in responsibilities for your current role or be willing to accept a different role altogether if presented with the opportunity. The world tends to be short on volunteers. Sometimes being competent, in the right place at the right time, and being willing to say yes is all it takes for major career growth. Based on my experiences thus far, people who say yes to new opportunities tend to get more of them. When you say no, people tend to stop asking, and you can miss out on a lot. Obviously not every job offer should be accepted, but I would encourage you to let your default answer be yes and only change it if you can make a very strong case for it. Try evaluating internal job change opportunities by how much they will increase your internal value rather than just how pleasant they sound. Do not let the difficulty level of a role be a turn off. The more challenging the better, in my opinion. Just make sure that the hiring manager is aware of any concerns you have and has a mentoring and training plan in place. If the company is presenting you with the opportunity, then it is in their interest to help you succeed. Take advantage and be known as the type of person who can take on challenges with a good attitude and get up to speed quickly.

Increase your external value.
Over the course of your career, you will probably also experience a lot of change in your personal life. Sometimes you will need to move to support a spouse's career. Sometimes your company will restructure, and your position will be eliminated. Sometimes you will simply need a change of pace and some new challenges. In any case, you never want to find yourself on the hunt for a job without a marketable skill set. It is not your employer's job to make sure that you are valuable outside the organization, so this responsibility will mostly fall on you.

About five months after I started my first job, the company went through some financial issues and started a massive round of layoffs. It was a terrifying experience, but I was fortunate enough to retain my employment. I was on a dedicated team for a three year project, and as the project started wrapping up, I realized that my job might once again be in jeopardy. When I started updating my resume, I noticed that I had done an absolutely horrible job at making myself marketable to the outside world. I had little bits of experience in a bunch of different technologies and a lot of experience with a custom application used only by my company. Fortunately for me, I was offered another position at the same company after the project ended, but the whole experience was a wakeup call that changed my view on personal development.

After that first experience, I have consistently volunteered to work on anything new and accepted positions that allowed me to develop skill sets I did not already possess. It is a balancing act, but you should be able to find ways to contribute that help your organization while also helping you develop into the type of employee you want to be. There is usually no shortage of opportunities, so make sure you know where you want to end up, and then volunteer for assignments that help you get there.

Try to evaluate yourself objectively when it comes to your marketability. Know what you want to be and what you uniquely bring to the table. Once you have that figured out, be honest with yourself and identify any areas that would keep a hiring manager from giving you a chance. If there are not opportunities to work on filling your skill gaps at work, then make the time to address them outside of work. There are plenty of great resources, and the extra time is worth the investment.

A key part of being an exemplary employee is being well rounded at whatever it is that you do. This makes you more marketable to the outside world, but it also makes you more valuable internally. Being up to date on everything the outside world is doing allows you to contribute more in your current role and to propose changes that keep your organization as a whole more current and doing things more efficiently.

Here are two pieces of advice that will help you keep yourself marketable:

1. **Keep an eye on the market outside your organization.** No matter what industry you are in or how happy you are with your job, you should regularly be looking at external job postings. It is very easy to go heads down in your own organization and completely miss big changes in demand externally. Specifically look at job listings from companies that are leaders in your industry. Pay close attention to what they are looking for and make sure you have relevant experiences for the types of positions you might be interested in. Equally important to figuring out what you want out of your career is leaning what skills are needed. Meetups, email lists, and message boards are great ways to see what people in your industry are interested in and trying to learn. Let that guide your own learning. Also keep an eye out for ideas that you can propose to your supervisor or team. Outside perspective can often be lacking but provides a lot of value.
2. **If you don't have time to get where you need to be between 8 and 5, do it after.** Working after work is not fun, but sometimes it is necessary. If you know that the jobs you are interested in require skills in JavaScript development but you have a role in database administration, then do not expect to learn JavaScript at work. Find some learning resources online (pay for them if you need to), and then dedicate a couple of two hour blocks throughout the week to work through them. Also, pick a toy project that you can put in a public space (GitHub, a WordPress site, whatever). Make sure that it is out there and available before you start applying anywhere. If your work history does not have experience in a specific skill, then make sure your potential hiring manager can see your work. This carries much more weight than simply saying that you have been working on

it in your spare time.

Here is a personal example of how I have applied this advice:

A few years ago, my wife accepted a job opportunity in a different state. I moved with her and was allowed to work remotely for a short time to hand off responsibilities. Since I knew my time was limited and that I would need to start applying for jobs soon, I started by making a list of my current skills and experiences and then looking at job postings for the location where I had moved. I noticed pretty quickly that the skills on the job listings could be divided into three categories: things I have direct experience with, things where I have experience with something similar, things I have no experience with.

Regarding the things I had experience with, I did not really need to do anything extra. For the areas where I had experience with similar things, I started reading about the specific technologies that were listed on the job postings so that I could discuss the differences if asked in an interview. For example, at the time I had experience using Git with TFS, but most companies that were hiring wanted GitHub experience. I was able to learn enough about GitHub to say confidently that my skills would translate.

The hardest part was figuring out how to approach the areas where I had no experience. I picked what seemed to be the two or three most prevalent technologies and purchased relevant online training classes. I also wrote tools (on my own time) that would be useful for my current coworkers (and others) using those new technologies and then put them on GitHub. It was a lot of work, but it paid off, and I found a job very quickly. I am thankful that I took steps to make myself more marketable while I was still employed rather than waiting until I started interviewing and realizing then that I had limiting weaknesses.

Putting it all together.
Every job is different, and what is useful for you to know will vary. There will, however, always be opportunities to increase your own value as an employee (or as a prospective employee). Set aside time dedicated to increasing your value with consideration for both the things going on inside your company and what the market outside is doing. Over time, you will probably learn a lot about the most efficient way to do this, so do not be afraid to change things up as you have new ideas. The important thing is that you do it consistently.

8. Share The Success

Disclaimer: The concepts that will be discussed in this chapter are the types of things you can start thinking about once you have a solid handle on the specific skills needed for your job, where your job fits in relation to the rest of your team, and where your team fits in relation to the rest of the company. These are not things you should be worried about implementing early in your career or on your first day in a new role. It is great perspective to have in mind as you learn, but you will be very limited in your effectiveness if you try to start influencing your coworkers before you have the knowledge and experience to do it well.

Aside from getting things done, communicating well, etc., exemplary employees help get the most out of the people around them. It is in the interest of any company to have a strong, constantly improving workforce. Many employees focus entirely on their own job and performance. A good way to differentiate yourself as someone who goes above and beyond is to help find ways to get the most out of your coworkers. In sports reporting, it is often said that the greatest players elevate the performance of the team around them. It should be your goal to have that reputation at work.

In the previous chapter (Never Stop Making Yourself More Valuable), we talked about understanding the big picture of your organization and how things get done. Another part of this is understanding the full scope of what your team needs to do across different projects and initiatives. It is very easy to get bogged down in whatever assignment you are currently working on, but next level performance comes from being able to periodically step back and evaluate how to best deploy your team to efficiently work toward success on all fronts.

I have no desire to be a C-level executive. I like being hands on with the work that I do. I do not need to climb the corporate ladder to get what I want out of my career. What I have found most rewarding over my years in the workforce is helping others develop, helping teams succeed, and being given regular opportunities to take on new challenges that require learning something new. Having a mindset that emphasizes team success rather than self-promotion has consistently set me up to meet all of these goals.

Here are some more specific examples of ways to share the success:

Be a team player.
As mentioned in previous chapters, the way I conduct myself in the workplace is often determined by observing others and trying to mimic the traits I like and eliminate the traits I do not. There are a lot of people who are in it entirely for themselves and focus only on personal success. I generally do not enjoy working with those people. There are, thankfully, also a lot of people who are incredibly kind, intelligent, and generous with their time. I have been fortunate enough to work with a number of people over the years who are willing to teach, help, and mentor. Those are the people I want to model myself after.

Being a team player is really pretty easy. All that it requires is making time for others, making yourself (reasonably) available to help out, and being willing to occasionally do some work that you will not get direct credit for. Over time, though, team players have a better reputation across teams, better working relationships with their own team, and more organizational value than people who focus only on their own accomplishments. If you have followed the advice in the previous chapters of this book, then you should be (or at least be working toward being) in a place where you understand the larger goals and priorities for your team. When you can then leverage that understanding into being adaptable and helping your team succeed on the most important things, then you are taking a big step toward being one of your company's best assets.

If this is a new concept to you or you have not been fortunate enough to work with others who are good at it, then an easy way to get started is to work with your supervisor to create performance goals that directly encompass contributions to team success. It is good to go into that type of discussion with some ideas in mind, but be open to suggestions and incorporate any feedback your supervisor may have. This is yet another opportunity to understand their perspective and priorities. I have never received negative feedback when asking for advice on how to better support my coworkers and contribute to team success.

You can also start small. I have never started working on a team that had a good onboarding process. There usually is not a single list of tools to install, there are always permissions that have not been set up, and no one ever seems to know who can grant access to the things a new employee needs. Being new to the team (and not having access) usually means there are a couple of days where I am spinning my wheels. I always use that time to create onboarding documentation so that the experience goes more smoothly for the next person who comes in. This is a very minor example, but it shows how you can always find things to do to benefit the team.

Another example is from a previous job where everyone was horribly overworked. Our very small team was handling four projects at once, and they all had very aggressive deadlines. The team was made up of people with vastly different experience levels, and everyone was in over their head. I noticed that the stressful environment was leading to everyone being in silos and feeling like they were completely on their own when issues arose on their project. To address this, another senior team member and I started having "office hours". Every afternoon we would go to a conference room for an hour, and anyone who had issues, questions, or ideas to kick around was welcome to join us. If anyone stopped by, we would give them our undivided attention. If no one came by, we would just use the time to work on our own stuff. Communication improved, and people spent less time being blocked by technical challenges.

This did not in any way help us get our own work done faster. No project manager gave us a bonus because of it. There were occasions when sacrificing that time meant we had to work extra time in the evening to make up for it. However, the "office hours" were a tremendous help to the team and helped us all deliver better across the board. It also vastly improved the working relationships on our team and reversed the siloing trend that was starting to develop. Our supervisor could not have been more pleased.

Create opportunities for others.
If you are anything like me, then the longer you are in a role the longer your to-do list becomes. There are a million little ideas for tools, clean up tasks, and process improvements that you may or may not ever have time to actually investigate. For the first few years of my career, I would always work on these projects at the end of the year when everyone else was out of the office. Over time, though, I have begun to use my slack time differently.

Now when I have free time at the end of the year, instead of fully implementing something from my to-do list, I will write documentation, do a small proof of concept (just enough to prove it will work), and then hand it off to someone else to implement. I can usually get a couple of these done in a week or two, and then I make sure and give them to someone who would uniquely benefit from the experience. What I have learned is that it is not the most efficient use of my time to do something that is a simple variation on something I have done a million times before. It is also not sustainable for me to be the owner and primary contact for all of the custom tools that my team uses and maintains. Handing these small projects off creates easy wins for other team members and allows them to develop a sense of ownership around something the team does.

"I told someone else to implement something cool" is not something you would ever write in your end of year performance results, but that is okay. When your ideas are implemented, knowledge is spread across the team, and responsibility for team processes is divided up efficiently, then the whole team benefits (including you). Rather than adding something else to the list of things you support, you have solved a problem and empowered a coworker. Over the course of your career, you really do not need to take credit for every initiative that you help push through. People on the outside will notice that the teams you join get better, and that is a great reputation to have.

Putting it all together.
Although most of the examples in this chapter come from the perspective of someone who is later in their career with a lot of experience, the mindset is relevant at any point. I would encourage you to keep team success at the front of your mind. At different points in your career, this will mean different things, but setting up others to succeed and maintaining good working relationships with the people around you is always doable and is never something you will regret.

9. Cultivate Good Relationships And Communication

As mentioned in the previous chapter, exemplary employees improve the environment around them. Communication is often one of the biggest barriers to progress and efficiency. An organization can be packed full of wildly talented people, but if they cannot communicate and coordinate, they will never reach their full potential for productivity. Having well defined processes is great. Having clearly documented requirements is awesome. Without good communication, though, a team is not set up for success.

There are many reasons that people fail to communicate effectively. Some people feel so overwhelmed by their workload that they do not even have time to think about it. Others have spent their careers working in isolation and do not know any other way. Sometimes organizations are structured in a way that is not conducive to collaboration. All of these are things I have seen in my career. None of them are impossible to overcome.

As a quick aside, I feel like I should probably mention that some people actively choose to not communicate or share their knowledge. In my experience, this has typically been an issue that management has addressed in one way or another. When working with someone who refuses to communicate, do not get too bogged down. Give them every opportunity to contribute, but do not be discouraged if they refuse to do so. Supervisors are there for a reason, and this is one of those things they are uniquely positioned to address.

In general, your career should be spent identifying areas of weakness and strengthening them. A good way to improve things for everyone is to identify and fill communication gaps. Learn to be a good facilitator. Look around at the people you work with and see what works and what does not. Identify people who are good communicators and learn from them. Be sensitive to the situation and personalities involved, and do what you can to make everyone feel comfortable contributing.

Here are some tactics for improving relationships and communication that have worked well for me:

Form good relationships.
It is tremendously helpful to get to know the people around you on a personal level. Work is more fun when you are doing it with friends, and when pressure mounts and stress levels rise, it is good to not have the relationship based entirely on the work environment. Personal relationships lead to more openness and honesty, and both sides benefit from it. FIgure out what makes people feel comfortable with contributing in meetings, and then do your best to create that type of environment for them. Figure out what keeps people from contributing in meetings and eliminate it. Remember birthdays and be sensitive to other people's personal lives. Invest in your relationships with people inside and outside your team, and you will reap the benefits every day. Communication will naturally improve when relationships are solid.

It is really, really easy to get caught up in the shuffle and feel overwhelmed by your workload. Many times the more you know about your job, the more things you realize that need to get done. A whole organization of people with that mindset can lead to a culture of "not my problem". You will stand in stark contrast to those around you if you are known as a person who will make time to help other people. Exemplary employees get things done, and they also help others get things done. This benefits the whole organization.

I have never been the smartest or most talented person in any room. In order to offset this, I work hard, treat people with respect, and do my best to help people when they ask for it. When someone asks me for something that I cannot do, I make it a point to never say "That's not my job", "I don't know", or "Ask someone else". Instead, I do my best to understand the request fully, explain what all is involved in completing the request (to my knowledge), and then direct the requestor to the specific person or people who can accomplish the request. Then I follow up with them a day or two later to make sure that they have everything they need to move the task along. This absolutely takes extra effort on my part, and it is not something that shows up in my yearly performance results. The benefit of this approach is that it helps the team function more effectively and tends to result in great relationships with those around me.

Relationships are a two way street. When other people go out of their way to help you, make sure they know you appreciate it. Over the years I have regularly sent candy bars, cookies, thank you notes, and gift cards to coworkers who have gone above and beyond to help me out. I also send a lot of emails to supervisors of other teams to let them know when one of their employees does something awesome. Everyone responds best to different things, but regularly find ways to let others know that you appreciate it when they help you.

Make everyone feel represented and heard.
The best teams are ones where everyone contributes. No matter differences in skill level, background, or personality, there is no reason that someone on your team should not be engaged and contributing on a regular basis. People typically feel a stronger sense of ownership when they are part of the decision, and they tend to work harder on an approach that they helped define. More eyes on a problem tend to be more likely to spot potential issues. More people involved in defining a process often results in a process that benefits everyone equally.

There are a lot of reasons why people do not contribute to the discussion, but you should be on the lookout for ways to enable everyone to be involved. Some people would prefer to research and document a topic than to present about it in a meeting. Others do better one on one than in groups. Whatever it takes, do what you can to help your team members express their ideas. Work with them to create an environment where they can be part of the team discussion. Be willing to change the process if needed.

One on one talks before meetings.
One area where communication often needs the most improvement is in meetings. I cannot count the number of times that I have entered a meeting with no idea what would be covered or what was expected from me. This does not lay the groundwork for a productive discussion. In a conference room with a short timeline is not the best way to do research or design a good solution. I know I am not doing my best work or providing the best feedback when I am solving a problem I have only known about for a few minutes with no investigation or context. When you have an entire room of people in that same boat, you will rarely end up with the best path forward. Also, when there are dissenting opinions, the person with the loudest voice tends to win because no one has been given time to investigate.

In order to avoid these types of situations, I have often invested time before large project meetings in one on one sessions with project resources from other teams. I talk to them about what they are envisioning for their implementation and how they see it integrating. I ask what their assumptions are for what my team would provide and talk through any risks or unknowns. By the time we get to an actual meeting with a project manager, I like for everyone to have had a chance to raise questions and investigate their ideas. This means a lot of non-ideal options will have already been eliminated, and everyone is already thinking about how the project implementation will work across teams. While this does involve some additional time spent on my part, I feel like it pays off enough to be worth it without question.

Do not be reluctant to apologize.
No one is perfect, and everyone makes mistakes. Not everyone is willing to admit it, though, and even fewer people actually follow through and apologize when they should. One thing that will set you apart from the average employee is a humble attitude. A lot of people seem to be under the impression that it is a sign of weakness to take responsibility when things do not go well. Personally, I think that it is a sign of insecurity when someone will not admit their mistakes.

You probably know someone who constantly blames others for their failures and never owns up to any of their shortcomings. That attitude does not make for a good team member, a good employee, or a high performer. When (not if) you make a mistake, but sure to take responsibility. Do not blame others, and focus on what you can learn from it.

Here are some things you can do the next time you make a mistake at work:

1. Understand what went wrong and why.
2. Identify the lesson you can learn and something you can do differently in the future to avoid making the mistake again.
3. Admit your mistake to the people who need to know. It is much better that they hear it from you.
4. Apologize and share your plan to prevent it from happening again.

If you follow these steps, then you will normally come out of the situation still looking trustworthy and responsible.

One final note: If you do something that hurts someone else on a personal level, then apologize to them in person in a meaningful way and in a timely manner. At the end of the day, work is temporary. Personal relationships are more important. Your project deadline can wait while you repair a damaged relationship with a coworker.

Participate in community events.
The office Christmas party. The monthly birthday event in the break room.

YOUR CAREER SUCKS

The office volleyball league. You have seen the flyers. You have received (and ignored) the emails from the party planning committee. It seems like there is always something non-work-related going on that is attempting to distract you from your goal of getting your work done and going home.

Over the last several years, I have noticed that "company culture" is a bigger and bigger area of focus. I am not sure if the focus is actually increasing or if I have just become more aware of it, but it seems like every corporate website has multiple pages about their culture and values. It seems to be very important to companies to foster a sense of community among employees. My guess is that they see it as helping improve retention, but whatever the reason, organizations value it, so it is something you should pay attention to.

When a company values something, it tends to reward it. On the list of things you can do that add value to your career, participating in events that someone else plans is one of the easier ones. It gives you positive visibility to management and has the added benefit of helping you to meet people outside your normal circle. You never know who in the company you will end up working with on a project, and investing in your relationships with coworkers is never going to hurt you in the long run. In fact, it is an essential part of long term career success.

By no means am I encouraging you to take part in every event. If you spend all day socializing rather than doing work, then that will not be good for your reputation. It is worth your time, however, to pick a few events throughout the year and get involved. There are bound to be at least a few that line up well with your interests. Join the office fantasy football league. Spend a day volunteering with your coworkers at Habitat for Humanity. Bring cookies to the potluck. Wear an ugly sweater to the Christmas party.

For extra credit, volunteer to help organize something once in a while. There is usually a shortage of people willing to help make something social happen in the office, so a little volunteering can go a long way. If you typically do not care for the types of events that go on at your workplace, then volunteer and start something new that would appeal to your interests. You probably will not be alone in your thinking and may meet some new friends in the process.

Finally, I know that not everyone is comfortable in group settings or with attending an event full of strangers. Being shy is okay, and it is not something that has to hinder your career. Personally, I do much better in one on one conversations than group discussions. One of the best ways to help make large events more pleasant is to invite someone from your group to attend with you. Odds are that there are people you already know who would be willing to attend office events but do not simply because they feel like they would be doing it alone. I will often send out an email just to my team to see if anyone else is interested in attending something that I do not particularly want to attend on my own. I almost always find someone else who is willing to go, and then we both have a better time because of it.

Putting it all together.
Every work environment is different and has its own unique set of personalities and quirks. You will need to learn these things and then figure out how to navigate them effectively. First attempts are never perfect, so do not get discouraged. Just keep trying things until something works. You will never be best friends with everyone in the company, but there is no reason not to have a good working relationship with your coworkers. Be humble and do what you can to get everyone involved and working together. Make time to get out of your comfort zone and interact with people you have not met yet.

10. Respect Everyone's Time

Exemplary employees respect everyone else's time. There will be a lot of overlap between this chapter and some previous ones, but I felt like this point was important enough to focus on it specifically for a few pages. Time is a fixed quantity. You cannot buy more of it. You cannot slow it down or speed it up by choice. It is something that we are all a part of but have no control over. On a day by day basis, we each choose how to allocate the limited amount of time that we have. Those choices impact our careers, our health, and our personal lives. Managing time is difficult to begin with, and how well we do it has effects that cascade into many other areas of life. Time is important, and that is why it is tremendously important to respect the fixed amount of it that other people have.

As mentioned several times previously, a lot of what I do at work is based on not treating others in ways that I do not like to be treated. When I am at work, I maintain an internal sense of urgency for making progress. This increases or decreases based on organizational need, project timelines, or problems that need to be fixed, but I generally spend my time working against an aggressive timeline that I set for myself for each task. This means that when I am at work, I am rarely bored, and I rarely leave at the end of the day feeling like I got everything done that needed to get done. As my career has progressed and I have held positions with more responsibility, this has been magnified. When I am at work, I am on a mission, and it is more than enough to keep me busy from when I arrive in the morning until when I leave in the evening.

The office is (and should be) a collaborative place. Even as a developer, I have never worked in an environment that did not include multiple daily conversations and meetings with stakeholders, team members, and coworkers from other departments. This is absolutely necessary and part of the job. In these daily interactions, though, there are countless opportunities to (on purpose or not) claim time from other people in a way that is not productive. This wastes the limited amount of time they have and keeps them from accomplishing their goals in a timely manner. It is an absolutely terrible feeling to be at work late wrapping up a task that you could not complete during normal working hours because someone else was disrespectful of your time during the day.

"Wasting time" is hard to define. A junior member of the team asking me for clarity on a particular task after they have already made an honest attempt to complete it is not a waste of time. Someone from another team asking me for helping troubleshooting an issue that spans across our areas of responsibility is not a waste of time. A product manager bouncing an idea for a new feature off of me before going to a meeting and presenting it to project stakeholders is good for both of us. Rather than continuing to say vague things like "Thou shalt not time waste", the rest of this chapter will be focused around some good habits that are centered on respecting your coworkers' time and avoiding the things that I have seen be issues in this area most often.

For meetings, set an agenda and stick to it.
Meetings are the bane of my existence. I enjoy working with other people to design and implement solutions. I like getting everyone on the same page and directing our efforts in a complementary direction. I do not like is spending fifteen to twenty minutes trying to get everyone into the same screen sharing session and conference line. I do not like unstructured and undirected time with a large number of people and no agenda. I REALLY do not like having the same meeting more than once.

A lot of meeting organizers seem to think that if they can just get all the right people in a room together then problems will magically solve themselves. The downfall of this is that when there is no formal agenda or set of goals, then everyone is going to try and direct the conversation toward their own interests and concerns. This typically results in meetings that run long and accomplish little. I have also noticed that engagement tends to be lower in these types of meetings. When the discussion is not focused, then you tend to have a lot of people who are on their laptops or phones and not contributing unless they are directly asked about something. When you do not respect someone else's time, they do not respect yours. All in all, unstructured meetings shape up to be colossal wastes of time.

Meetings are difficult to manage successfully, but they are important. Coordinating efforts across teams, organizations, project teams, or even the whole company allows you to tap into a whole different level of productivity than you would by merely having people contribute individually from their own silos. The more people that are involved, though, the more effort it takes to keep things organized. A meeting agenda with clear goals and expectations that everyone is aware of ahead of time is a good place to start. Setting a time limit and sticking to it is a good way to keep things on track as well. In general, I feel like you get out of a meeting what you put into it. More work on the front end pays off.

While you cannot control meetings that other people schedule, you can control your own. Here are some specific things you can do for every meeting you organize to keep things on track and respect everyone else's time:

1. **Understand the purpose of the meeting:** Before you schedule anything, you should have a very clear understanding of what you are trying to accomplish. Put in the effort to figure out your goals, and then do the research to fully understand it.
2. **Figure out who needs to be there:** Once you know what you are trying to accomplish, then spend some time thinking about who really needs to be there to help. Talk to supervisors or project managers if you need to, but make sure that everyone you invite is either someone who can help you accomplish your goal or who will be affected by the details of it.
3. **Set a detailed agenda:** You cannot expect everyone who attends your meeting to magically know what you expect from them. It is also very difficult to direct a flowing conversation and make sure that it eventually addresses all of your needs and concerns. People are very unlikely to self-regulate the length of discussions to make sure that there is enough time for everything you want to cover if they do not know an agenda.
4. **Communicate the agenda:** An agenda does not do any good if no one sees it. Send it out far enough ahead of time that everyone has time to ask questions and do prep work.
5. **Set things up ahead of time:** Once everyone is in the room and ready to start is the worst possible time to try and figure out conference line or screen sharing issues. Take care of this ahead of time so that all of the time spent in the meeting can be focused on meeting the goals in your agenda.
6. **Keep things on track:** During the meeting, make sure that the discussion stays on track. If things start to go in a different direction, then offer to schedule a separate meeting to address other concerns.
7. **Stick to your time limit:** If the meeting is productive and on target and you simply do not have time to cover everything on your agenda,

then ask if everyone wants to continue. If any of the attendees have a conflict, then schedule a follow up at a later time.

Also, this is entirely optional, so do not take it as gospel, but I personally find that it helps to dress up a little if you are leading a meeting. Whether consciously or unconsciously, I think that the way you dress sets the tone of how other people view you. If you are going to lead a meeting, then it is probably not a bad idea to wear something at the nicer end of what is normal for your office. I think that it shows you take the meeting seriously and are there with a specific purpose in mind. Maybe it is all in my head, but it seems like it works in my experience.

Show up on time every time.
Whether for team meetings, project touchpoints, or one on ones, people constantly waste each other's time in the workplace by showing up late. Do not be the reason that someone has to restart a meeting. Do not be the reason that one of your coworkers sits alone in a conference room for ten minutes waiting on you when they could spend that time doing something more productive. Do not be the person that keeps the carpool from leaving for the day. Being punctual communicates to others that you value their time and also take your own time management seriously.

Be aware of others.
Socializing in the office is important. Having good working and personal relationships with the people around you is vital. It makes you more productive, and it also makes your day significantly more enjoyable on every level. One important thing to realize about socializing in the office, though, is that different people have different needs and preferences. You should be extra aware of others when you are in the office, and make sure that the time you spend interacting with them is both welcome and respectful of their time.

You cannot read the minds of your coworkers. Even though you may not be busy, that does not mean they are not. Different people are on different timelines. Different people have different sets of responsibilities both inside and outside of work. Socializing is great, but make sure it does not come at the cost of someone else working late or being annoyed with you.

Some people are too polite to say "I am really busy right now, will you please leave me alone?", so it is up to you to be sensitive to their interactions. If someone keeps facing their computer as you talk to them, it is probably not a good time to talk. If someone is not asking questions or adding to the discussion, then they probably want it to end. If they start to move away, then let them go. In general, do not make a habit of driving a conversation in the office past ten to fifteen minutes. If the other person is actively engaged at that point, then it is fine to continue - just be sure to provide periodic chances to gracefully disengage.

Although I am sure this would not apply to anyone reading this book, I think it is worth mentioning that some people choose to waste their own time at work. Whether they are counting down the days until retirement, are distracted by an upcoming vacation, or simply are not interested in starting a new task thirty minutes before leaving for the day, some people have no interest in doing anything productive and are merely waiting out the clock. It is one thing to make that choice for yourself, but if you do, then at least have the courtesy to not force it on anyone else.

Make the most of it when others help you.
When someone else is willing to invest some of their time to help you, then make sure that you make it as effective as possible. I never mind answering a question for a coworker when it is something they have no way of knowing how to do and me walking them through it saves a lot of time. What can get annoying, though, is having to answer the same question over and over. As mentioned in previous chapters, when someone takes the time to teach me something, I make a habit of documenting it and then sending it back to them for review so that they do not have to spend time answering the same question again for me (or anyone else) in the future. When someone helps me troubleshoot an issue, I make a habit of documenting the solution and also thanking them in public. I understand that everyone else's time is valuable, and when they are willing to use some of it to help me out, then I do my best to make it as effective as possible.

Putting it all together.
We all spend a lot of time in the office, and we all have lives outside the office. One of the best ways to keep good relationships with your co-workers is to be respectful of their time. As mentioned several times already, think about team success and enabling others to do what they need to do so that they can manage their own time and not have it managed by you. I am generally a fan of the Golden Rule, and time is important to me. I respect other people's time and in that way politely ask them to respect mine.

11. Know When To Make A Change

So far, all the chapters in this book have focused on actions you can take to help yourself provide value, improve the perception that others have of you, and build a strong reputation. While all of this effort certainly makes you deserving of career advancement, it does not guarantee it. Promotions, bonuses, and new opportunities all require a lot of people beyond just yourself to take action on your behalf. There are many reasons why you may be doing everything right but still not seeing the payoff in your career.

Every company has different philosophies for how to manage internal development. Some companies are clingy and like to promote internally at any cost. Others tend to treat employees more like commodities and always buy at the cheapest price. Despite what a company says about its own philosophy on career progression, it is important to pay attention to what is actually happening and how well that fits with your own goals. Actions speak louder than words, and a company tells you a lot by who and how it rewards and advances. Make sure you have a realistic understand of how it the process works.

The way a company usually measures its own value is by how profitable it is. Whether it is publicly traded or not, every business must maintain a budget that it can afford. There are many different schools of thought about how to allocate that budget, and some of them are more conducive to employee advancement than others. Make an effort to understand what your company values. Money follows value, and if your position is not in an area that is valued, then your career advancement may be limited. Keep an eye on the outside world. There are almost always job opportunities where you could be doing something that the organization values.

It feels silly to have to say this, but don't forget that your individual happiness is also extremely important. In the hustle of the day to day, it can be easy to stay so focused on your job tasks and career that you can lose sight of the health and happiness of the rest of your life. The whole point of this book is to help you work more effectively and be less stressed so that you can have a great career that allows you enjoy the other parts of your life that you find most fulfilling. If the organizational structure, team dynamic, or internal processes at your company are preventing that, then get out!

If you work at a company where you are doing everything in this book and are not experience sustained career growth, or if you are consistently finding yourself feeling frustrated and deflated at the end of the day, then be open to change. The same habits and drive that make you worthy of promotion in your current role will easily translate to other jobs as well. If you care enough about your career to be reading this book, then you are already demonstrating a level of self-awareness and motivation to invest in yourself that most people do not have. Change is scary, but don't be afraid to bet on yourself and explore new opportunities.

Here are some ways to keep a good feel on your value both inside and outside your organization:

Reassess your situation regularly.
Life is busy, and it is so easy to get completely caught up in the day to day. It takes deliberate effort to take a step back and asses things objectively. Something that will be brought up a lot in this chapter is to develop a habit of devoting some time every six months reflecting on your current situation.

Here are some useful questions with which to start when taking inventory:

- Am I more or less happy than I was six months ago?
- Do I feel like my career is healthy?
- How much is work bleeding over into my personal life?
- Are my skills more or less marketable than they were six months ago?
- Am I regularly spending enough time on the things that are most important to me in life?
- Am I making enough that I don't have to lose sleep about money?
- Do you like spending 8+ hours per day with your coworkers?
- Do you feel like the work you do is valued at your company?
- Is management supporting you and your team?

Every job has stretches of time that are harder than others. There are also factors completely unrelated to your job that could be affecting your answer to the above questions. One bad report card is not always an indication of an unfixable problem. What is useful, though, is to track your answers to the above questions over time. If you have gone a full year without any of the answers improving, then that is probably a good indication that you may need to consider making a change in your employment situation.

Pay attention to your surroundings.
You are not the only person at your company. Even if things are going well for you, that does not mean that the organization is healthy. Sometimes you can spot potential issues or signs of trouble simply by observing others. When you are in a position of privilege, it is easy to be blind to the struggles of others, but those struggles can often inform you that it is time to start considering other opportunities before things start to get uncomfortable for you.

Here are some things to keep an eye on:

- **Who is getting promoted?** Is your company promoting people who are team players, or are they promotion people who play political games? Are other people who do similar work to yourself seeing continued success as they spend more time working for the company, or do they find themselves capping out?
- **How is your team viewed by the rest of the company?** Does your team have a reputation of providing value and being easy to work with, or is your team known for taking a long time to get things done and generally being difficult to interact with? Are you perceived as adding value or as being an expense? Are you problem solvers or a necessary evil?
- **How healthy is your team?** Is there mutual respect among team members and management? Does everyone feel like they are able to voice their ideas and contribute? Do teammates help each other achieve success? Is everyone working toward the same goals?
- **Is management actively trying to fix problems?** No team is perfect, but is management proactive about fixing issues, or do they prefer to let things play out and hope that bad situations naturally improve? Does management spend more time rewarding good behavior or ignoring bad behavior? Does your manager get along well with the managers from other teams? Does your manager represent you well to people at higher levels in the company?

If people are being rewarded for the wrong reasons, then you're probably never going to get promoted. If your team isn't seen as adding value to your company, then your potential for success is limited. If your team is unhealthy, then it's going to be hard to sustain any kind of success. If your manager doesn't support your team, then you're being set up to fail.

Monitor the job listings in your area.
It is tremendously useful to stay up to date on the job market. It doesn't cost anything to look at job postings, but they contain tons of useful information that can help you steer your career intelligently. Job sites like Indeed, Monster, Dice, and The Muse are great resources.

Here are some things you want to pay attention to when browsing job listings:

- **Trends:** What technologies, skills, tools, or experiences are other companies looking for? If there are skills that are becoming essential for your industry, then it is in your best interest to find ways to develop them. If you do not have the opportunity to do so in your current role, then find a way to do it outside of work. It's better to sacrifice a little time during your lunch break or on weekends than to not be able to find a job when you're ready.
- **Salary Ranges:** Many companies are notoriously bad about keeping employee salaries up to date with outside markets. By doing a little research, you may find that you are worth tens of thousands of dollars per year more than you are currently making. You may also find out that what you are making is actually very competitive for your industry and skill set. The grass isn't always greener.
- **Terminology:** Most industries are very quick to adopt new buzzwords. If you see a lot of vocabulary that you do not recognize in job listings for your industry, then it's time to do some research and get current. This also helps you know the proper terminology to use in your resume.
- **Availability:** For many reasons, most industries are somewhat cyclical. If jobs are not readily available in your industry, then it might not be the best time to consider a change. It never hurts to look or apply, but don't take a job that isn't a good career move just for the sake of change. Things can change pretty radically in the scope of just a few months. Get a feel for how the job market functions in your industry and geographical area.

As mentioned in a previous chapter, your company is not particularly concerned with making sure that you are remaining marketable to other companies. Your organization is also not motivated to tell you what people in your role make at other companies. All of the resources to obtain this information are out there, though, so take advantage of them. Use what you learn to help with your evaluation of your own situation.

Keep your resume up to date.
If you take nothing else from this book, then PLEASE start keeping your resume up to date. Resumes are not fun and nothing in life outside of actively looking for a job really forces you to update yours, so it's easy to just not do it. Much like the performance review process, your resume is something that is only as useful as you allow it to be. Since nothing is forcing you to do it, I would highly recommend creating a calendar reminder to prompt you to update your resume every six months and then prioritizing that task when it comes up.

Having an updated resume has three huge benefits:

1. It helps you monitor your own growth. If after six months you don't have any new skills or accomplishments to add to your resume, then something is wrong. If you are putting in the effort to do the things outlined in the previous chapters of this book and not seeing any new opportunities, then I would be very suspicious of your organization's internal talent evaluation and rewards process. Even if your company is not helping you move your career forward, though, there is no reason why you shouldn't be finding ways to acquire new skills on your own. Updating your resume is a good way to keep yourself honest on that front.
2. It helps you assess your own marketability. For me, the hardest part about maintaining a resume has always been how little room you have to make a case for yourself. It kind of hurts to have to distill my decade-worth of career experience and acquired skills into a single page of headings and bullet points. It is a valuable exercise, though, because it helps me see how a hiring company would see me. Generally when a job is posted, it's looking to solve a particular problem. Your resume should basically be a statement with supporting evidence about what sorts of problems you are uniquely qualified to be able to solve. Thinking in these terms should clarify what types of job opportunities could be available to you. If you're not happy with the answer, then you can start taking action to fill in the gaps.
3. You are always prepared if a great opportunity comes along. LIke it or not, very little career movement happens without an updated resume. Whether it's an internal employee profile, a formal resume, or a profile on a job site, your next major opportunity will likely involve it at some point. Make sure that yours is deliberate and polished. You never know who's looking. You also don't want to have to scramble to get one up to date or created if someone asks you

for one. You should always be ready to send someone a link to your resume immediately upon request.

Your resume is a great tool for evaluating yourself and your situation. Keeping it up to date is a pain, but if you do it regularly and make the most of it, then it provides a lot of value. Your resume could be the key to your next big career move, so give it the attention that it deserves.

Never be afraid to interview.
Interviewing is a skill, and you don't get good at it unless you practice. It doesn't cost anything to interview, and you can learn a lot from it. Most companies are terrible at writing job listings, and an actual interview usually reveals a thousand times more about what the company is actually looking for in a candidate. At some point, you will hopefully have the opportunity to interview for a job that is an awesome opportunity for your career and a great fit for your skills. It would be good if you went into that interview polished and prepared. Recent interviewing experience helps that happen.

When interviewing, be professional. Do not imply that you know things that you don't. Do not put anything on your resume that isn't accurate or that you aren't comfortable talking about. Respond to all communications in a timely manner. Be available in a quiet place at the agreed upon time for phone calls. Show up early for in-person meetings. Provide any information that is requested of you as quickly as possible. Even if you do not end up working with the company, you can still leave a good impression on them. There's always a chance that could pay off in the future.

I have heard a lot of people say they don't want to apply for a job because they don't think they would pass the interview. My advice has always been that it's better to let them tell you no than than to not give them the opportunity to say yes. Make sure that your resume is an accurate reflection of your skills and know what value you can uniquely bring to a company. Apply on those terms, and then be transparent about what you do and don't know. If a company does not choose to hire you for a particular job today, that doesn't mean that their experiences with you can't positively impact the situation if you apply for a different role with them in the future.

Finally, never be afraid to say no to a job offer. The job hunt process is very complicated and there are a million factors that go into employment decisions on both sides. If you get an offer and choose not to accept it, then be transparent about why, thank the company for their time, wish them luck in filling the role, and (if appropriate) let them know that you will keep them in mind if your situation changes in the future.

Putting it all together.
To be honest, this has been the most uncomfortable chapter of the book to write. I am naturally loyal to a fault and risk averse. I tend to undervalue my own skills and blame myself when things aren't going well. This whole chapter has been an exercise in writing down exactly the types of things I'm good at telling others but bad at putting into practice myself. I'm not saying that any of this is easy, but I do know that it's good advice.

If you are someone who regularly goes above and beyond in your job, supports your coworkers, makes an effort to stay current with your skills, sets others up for success, makes an effort to be transparent in your communication, and helps to make your manager's life easier, then you are are rare breed. Whether your company sees it or not, you are a tremendous asset. Do not sell yourself short. Do not be afraid to bet on yourself. If you are unhappy at work, then you deserve better. Don't hold yourself back.

Conclusion

Thank you so much for taking the time to read this book. As I mentioned in the introduction, it is the culmination of a lot of lessons I have learned the hard way over the course of my career. By going through the exercise of writing it all down, I feel like I have gained a lot of clarity on concepts that had been half-formed in the back of my mind for a long time. It is my sincerest hope that you can use the things that I have learned as a shortcut to quickly steer your career in the direction that you want and to find a fulfilling balance between work and home life. Best of luck!

Appendix

So far this book has covered a lot of different concepts. I did my best to give them some sort of logical organization, but really they all complement each other and the best results come from applying them together in different situations. The following sections will be devoted to giving examples of what that might look like for some common scenarios.

Meeting Scenario

Your team has been assigned a project that will require help from other teams to succeed. It is toward the end of the year, and you know people will be in and out for the holidays. You want to get ahead of the game and make sure that everyone knows what is needed from them and will be able to do what is needed for the success of the project.

Example Path Forward

Step 1: Identify who needs to be involved. You probably know who on your team should be there, but if not, then talk to your supervisor and find out. If you do not know who should be there to represent the other teams, then talk to their supervisors or your project manager to find out. Once you have the full list, then set up a meeting at a time when everyone who needs to be there (no more, no less) can attend.

Step 2: Create a meaningful meeting invite. Meeting invites should include enough information that everyone will understand why they are there when they get to the conference room. You should set the stage for why the meeting is happening, what will be covered, and what you would like to accomplish while you are there.

Step 3: Have any preparatory conversations that need to happen. If there is anyone who is invited to the meeting who does not have much background information on the project, then make a point to talk to them about what is going on ahead of time. If you are going to need information from them, then make sure they know that in advance and have time to research anything they need to look into.

Step 4: Create presentation materials. I hate PowerPoint. It is overused and easy to tune out. It is, however, wildly beneficial to be able to present your meeting agenda in a way that everyone is able to see. However you choose to accomplish this is fine. It is also usually a good idea to do a short introduction to explain the big picture of what is happening. Being able to show design diagrams or requirements documents can often be helpful. At a bare minimum, being able to display the meeting agenda and refer to it often is important, because it will help you manage time and keep things on track.

Step 5: Show up early. You should plan to be in the conference room 10-15 minutes before the meeting is scheduled to start. This will give you time to get set up and make sure that any conference call or display issues are resolved before everyone arrives.

Step 6: Keep things on track and take notes. When it is time for the meeting to start, do a short introduction that includes enough background information for everyone to be on the same page and a review of the agenda. Make sure that things stay on topic and productive, and make sure that you are moving along quickly enough to hit all of the topics on the agenda in the time that you have. Take lots of notes and make sure to capture specific action items and commitments and who they are associated with.

Step 7: Send a summary. As quickly as you can after the meeting, send out a summary email. Be sure to thank everyone for their time and also recap all action items and commitments and who they belong to.

NOTE: As mentioned in Chapter 10, I tend to dress up a little for meetings. It may seem unnecessary or outdated, but I feel like people take me more seriously if I wear something nicer than on the average day. I do think that people in general are conditioned to react to wardrobe, so you might as well use it to your advantage if you are trying to lead something.

Goal Setting Scenario

It is the beginning of the year, and you receive an email from HR that your performance goals must be set by the end of the month. Your supervisor sends a follow up email that she would like to meet with you next Monday to talk about your goals.

Example Path Forward

Step 1: Figure out where you want your career to go next. Personally, this is one of the hardest things for me. I feel like I do a good job of making the most of whatever situations I am in and at finding ways to keep myself interested and challenged. What I am not so good at is looking at the future and deciding what comes next. As mentioned in Chapter 5, a tool that I have found to be tremendously helpful for getting started is the company's list of salary grade expectations (or career ladder documentation or whatever formalized documentation they have about what is expected at different levels in the company). Look at whatever level you are currently at, and then base your goals around the things described for the next level. Also, if you have a long term goal of being a team lead or first time supervisor, then add something to your goals about developing the skills needed for that. You do not have to wait until the year that you want to do something to start preparing for it.

Step 2: Review your company's values and larger initiatives. Most companies have a list of core values or guiding principles. There are also usually several large, company-wide initiatives (going to the cloud, higher conversion rate from sales lead to customer, an increase in stock price, zero safety reportables, etc.). If you do not have a good grasp of either the values or initiatives, then talk to your supervisor or HR representative until you do.

Step 3: Write a solid first draft of your goals. Based on the information you gathered in Steps 1 and 2, start writing your goals. They do not have to be completely perfect, but they should be organized, clear, and thought-out. Align your goals with the larger company values and initiatives and make sure that accomplishing them will help make a case for your next personal career goal. Before the end of the day at least one business day before your review meeting (in this case, before the end of the day on the Friday before your Monday meeting), you should send a completed first draft to your supervisor. This gives her a chance to read through your goals and give them some thought before the meeting. The further in advance of the meeting you can get them to her, the better.

Step 4: Explain your goals to your supervisor. When you have your review meeting, start by explaining where you want to be in a year. Ask if that seems reasonable and then ask if there are any specific areas that would be good for you to focus on improving. Also be sure to ask for feedback on the rough draft that you submitted previously. These conversations are also a natural time to ask about any big projects or initiatives coming up in the next year that your supervisor sees as an especially high priority for the team and what she sees your role being in those projects. Be sure to take lots of notes. Note: If your supervisor does not set up a meeting with you to review your goals, be sure and take the initiative to set one up yourself.

Step 5: Incorporate feedback. The whole point of reviewing your goals with your supervisor is to facilitate a conversation about how you can work together to progress your career over the next year. Having your supervisor's buy in is essential for this to be successful. Make sure that you incorporate her feedback and then send your updated goals to her for review before the submission deadline.

Step 6: Submit your goals on time. Don't show up on the list of people who have not submitted their goals on time. This is an easy way to show your supervisor that you take the process seriously.

Demo Scenario

You have been working on a project for several months. Your supervisor asks you to demo where things are at currently for the project stakeholders.

Example Path Forward

Step 1: Figure out what is meaningful to your audience. There is no point in demoing something if it is not interesting or meaningful to your audience. If your project stakeholders are other people on your team, then showing things from your code editor and the command line is probably fine. If you are presenting to business managers, then you probably want to have something more visually appealing. In general, do your best to demo something in the same context that your audience will be interacting with it, and focus on the parts that they find interesting. If you are demoing to a project manager, then they probably do not care about seeing your individual code files. If you need to put in a little bit of extra effort to create some kind of visual interface for what you have been doing, then it is well worth the time.

Step 2: Establish context and tell a story. A good demo should be a story. It is not safe to assume that everyone in the room knows the intimate details of what you have been working on. It is generally a good idea to start with discussing the larger goals of your project and then using that as a frame of reference for the functionality that you are showing. This is especially true if the things you are showing off are more low level and less user-facing. Basically you should give enough context that your audience understands why what you are showing them matters. If nothing else, give them enough information to understand how what you have done gets them closer to having what they want.

Step 3: Prepare meaningful example data. Almost any demo is made significantly more compelling by using realistic example data. Your business audience may not understand data streaming architecture or containerization, but they definitely do understand business rules and how to apply them. If you can show real customer data being fed into your program and accurate results coming out, then that goes a long way toward establishing credibility and making your work relevant to your demo audience. If you are able to show that your results match those from an existing system, then that is even better.

Step 4: Show up early and do a dry run. It is a massive waste of time to gather a group of people in a room to show them something that does not work. It is also wildly unproductive for a group of people to sit around watching you try to troubleshoot an issue. If you are going to do a demo, then make sure that you show up early, step through the whole script on the machine that you will be using, and then fix any issues that arise. Also, make sure that you have your example data ready and easily accessible.

Step 5: Provide an update on what comes next. A demo is also a natural time to provide an update on the overall status of a project and what comes next. If you did a good job establishing context and telling the story of the project, then after you show what you have already done, you should easily be able to transition into a discussion on what comes next and when your audience can expect to see another demo. This helps establish trust, manage expectations, and also allows the stakeholders to provide any input on the project. It is much better to get their feedback early and often than all at once at the end of the project.

New Project Scenario

You are part of an internal web app development team at a large corporation, and you have been assigned to a new project that involves importing data from a legacy system, performing some business logic, and then displaying the results in interactive charts. The legacy system is supported by someone who is not on the project, and no one on the project has worked with it before. The business logic to be performed on the data is partially defined. There are mock ups for the interactive charts. Your company has a team that provides scheduling and monitoring for batch jobs. Your team does not have a go-to solution for interactive charting.

Example Path Forward

Obviously there are a lot of unknowns here. One of the hardest parts of any project is knowing where to start. One thing that will set you apart as exemplary is being able to step into a chaotic situation and then provide organization and start making progress.

Here is how I would approach this scenario:

Step 1 - Break it down into steps and classify each one: Begin by writing down all of the tasks you can think of that must be complete for the project to succeed. Then classify each one as either ready to work on or in need of additional research or clarification.
My initial list would look something like this:

- Ability to access legacy system. (Not ready - need to request from someone not on the project team)
- Ability to pull data from legacy system. (Not ready - need to explore data model once I have access)
- Local storage for transformed data. (Ready - just need to request a new database)
- Business logic for data from business units 1-3 (Ready)
- Business logic for data from business units 4-6 (Not ready - need answers on unclear requirements)
- Schedule the data export (Not ready - need clarification on how often it should be done and when it can be done without bogging down the old system)
- Investigate options for interactive charting (Ready)
- Develop charts for business units 1-3 (Not ready - will be ready when charting tool is chosen)
- Develop charts for business units 4-6 (Not ready - need answers on unclear requirements and to choose a charting tool)

Step 2 - Divide and conquer: For each of the steps above, figure out who is the best person to movie it forward. I may be capable of doing everything on the list, but the whole point of having a project team is to parallelize efforts.

This is how I would start moving forward:

- Schedule a meeting with the person who supports the legacy system to find out how to access it, if there are any times when we should avoid trying to pull data from it, and to learn more about the existing data model.
- Ask the project manager or product manager to provide additional clarity on business logic for data from business units 4-6 and scheduling the export.
- Ask whoever will own (and provide the PO for) the new database to request it.
- Start evaluating tools for charting.

Step 3 - Find ways to make incremental progress: I find a lot of value in seeing pieces of the project work end to end. I like to do a POC that prototypes my approach for solving the problem. In this case, I would probably start by finding a charting tool that I think will satisfy the business need and then write a quick example that uses it in conjunction with the business logic for whichever business unit has the simplest requirements. Rather than waiting on the new database or on getting access to the legacy system, I would create some example data on a local database on my machine and then just pull from that. After completing that piece, I would schedule a demo with the project stakeholders and get their feedback.

Step 4 - Make sure everyone is kept up to date on status: In addition to whatever task you are working on right now, make sure that everyone on the project team is kept aware of questions, risks, and incomplete requirements. A lot of times if you are making progress and doing demos, then everyone assumes that things are on track and that they do not really need to be doing anything. At least once a week, you should look back at the list you made in step one and report to your project manager any items that are still in "Not ready" status. If you burn through all the items that are ready to work on and then get stuck waiting for additional requirements, then that should not come as a surprise to anyone.

Step 5 - Handling the unexpected: There will always be unexpected challenges that get discovered over the course of a project. This is totally fine and not anyone's fault. The one word of caution that I will give is that when you find something that is significantly more complicated than you thought or that is an additional task that will need to be done for the project to succeed, then you should absolutely let your project team know as soon as possible. It is much better for everyone to know two months before a deadline that the project needs to be extended than it is to find out the night before.

YOUR CAREER SUCKS

www.ingramcontent.com/pod-product-compliance
Lightning Source LLC
Chambersburg PA
CBHW031447210526
45464CB00005B/2354